Exercising Essential Statistics

Second Edition

Evan M. Berman
Louisiana State University

CQ PRESS

A Division of Congressional Quarterly Inc.
Washington, D.C.

CQ Press
1255 22nd Street, NW, Suite 400
Washington, DC 20037

Phone: 202-729-1900; toll-free, 1-866-4CQ-PRESS (1-866-427-7737)

Web: www.cqpress.com

Cover design: Mike Grove, MG Design

∞ The paper used in this publication exceeds the
requirements of the American National Standard for Information
Sciences—Permanence of Paper for Printed Library Materials, ANSI Z39.48-1992.

Printed and bound in the United States of America

10   09   08   07   06   1   2   3   4   5

ISBN-10: 0-87289-332-4
ISBN-13: 978-0-87289-332-0

Screen shots reprinted by permission of the Microsoft Corporation.
SPSS User's Guide reprinted by permission of SPSS, Inc.

CONTENTS

Introduction...vi

Chapter One   Why Statistics for Public Managers and Analysts?
Q & A...1
Critical Thinking...2
Application Exercises..3
Further Reading...5

Chapter Two   Research Design
Q & A...6
Critical Thinking...8
Application Exercises..10
Further Reading...12

Chapter Three   Conceptualization and Measurement
Q & A...13
Critical Thinking...14
Application Exercises..16
Further Reading...18

Chapter Four   Measuring Performance: Present and Future
Q & A...19
Critical Thinking...20
Application Exercises..22
Further Reading...24

Chapter Five   Data Collection
Q & A...25
Critical Thinking...26
Application Exercises..28
Further Reading...30

Chapter Six   Central Tendency
Q & A...31
Critical Thinking...32
Data-Based Exercises..34
Further Reading...36

Chapter Seven   Measures of Dispersion

Q & A 37
Critical Thinking 38
Data-Based Exercises 40
Further Reading 43

Chapter Eight   Contingency Tables

Q & A 44
Critical Thinking 45
Data-Based Exercises 46
Further Reading 47

Chapter Nine   Hypothesis Testing with Chi-Square

Q & A 48
Critical Thinking 50
Data-Based Exercises 53
Further Reading 55

Chapter Ten   Measures of Association

Q & A 56
Critical Thinking 57
Data-Based Exercises 59
Further Reading 61

Chapter Eleven   The T-Test

Q & A 62
Critical Thinking 63
Data-Based Exercises 65
Further Reading 67

Chapter Twelve   Simple Regression

Q & A 68
Critical Thinking 69
Data-Based Exercises 70
Further Reading 71

Chapter Thirteen   Multiple Regression

Q & A 72
Critical Thinking 74
Data-Based Exercises 78
Further Reading 81

Chapter Fourteen   Logistic Regression

Q & A 82
Critical Thinking 83
Data-Based Exercises 84
Further Reading 86

Chapter Fifteen   Time Series Analysis

Q & A 87
Critical Thinking 88
Data-Based Exercises 90
Further Reading 94

apter Sixteen   Survey of Advanced Techniques
Q & A 95
Critical Thinking 96
Data-Based Exercises..98
Further Reading...99

apter Seventeen   SPSS User's Guide
SPSS Screens 100
Creating a Variable 100
Univariate Analysis: Means and Frequency Distributions...104
Variable Labels and Values..108
Defining Missing Values..113
Selecting a Subset of Observations for Analysis 113
Index Variables I: Cronbach Alpha...115
Index Variables II: Construction 118
Recoding Data 118
Hypothesis Testing with Chi-Square...126
T-Tests 128
Conclusion..129

apter Eighteen   Dataset Documentation
Public Perceptions 131
    General Description...131
    Methods..131
    Detailed Summary 131
    Note on Variables 131
    Survey Instrument: Orange County Citizen Survey...132
Employee Attitudes 136
    General Description...136
    Methods..136
    Detailed Summary 138
    Note on Variables 138
    Survey Instrument: Seminole County Government Employee Survey 138
Community Indicators...144
    General Description...144
    Definition of Variables..144
Watershed 146
    General Description...146
    Background 146
    Summary of Individual Variables: Condition Indicators 147
    Summary of Individual Variables: Vulnerability Indicators...148
Productivity 149
    General Description...149
    Background 149
    Summary of Variables...150
Crime 151
    General Description...151
    Background 152
    Explanation of Variables...152
Time 153
    General Description...153
    Summary of Variables...153

INTRODUCTION

This workbook is an integral part of the *Essential Statistics for Public Managers and Policy Analysts,* Second Edition, package. Whereas the textbook provides concepts and examples of statistical applications, the workbook further strengthens understanding by illustrating applications and encouraging analysts to think through statistical concepts in new and engaging ways. In short, the applications found here are key to mastering statistics.

Chapters 1 through 16 correspond to those in the textbook. The "Chapter Objectives" at the beginning of each textbook chapter are a good guide to what you will be practicing in each workbook chapter. To help students understand new concepts, four different sections are featured that target different aspects of learning. Specifically, each of these chapters is divided into the following sections:

- "Q & A" facilitates student learning of the statistical concepts through questions and answers. It is an ideal study guide for tests.
- "Critical Thinking" comprises short exercises to stimulate further conceptual insights into statistics and application
- "Application Exercises" in Chapters 1–5 or "Data-Based Exercises" in Chapters 6–16 help students develop hands-on skills using practical applications. The exercises in Chapters 6–16 draw on datasets provided on the accompanying CD.
- "Further Reading" lists work toward self-study in areas of interest to readers, including articles that students may w to access.

This workbook also includes chapters that extend the material covered in the textbook. Chapter 17 describes how to use SPSS, a statistical analysis program. It provides a step-by-step approach for ease of learning. Chapter 18 provide documentation for the datasets provided on the accompanying CD. The datasets are provided in SPSS, SAS, SYSTAT, and Stata formats for easy use. The SPSS datasets are compatible with the SPSS Student Version software.

The enclosed CD also provides bonus data and a complete report based on an actual citizen survey. The report a survey instrument are available electronically in Microsoft Word for your convenience. In addition, the CD includes a presentation in Microsoft PowerPoint, which will help users stretch their imaginations as they think of presenting the data to others in the public realm. A file discussing the use of spreadsheets in public management and analysis, including examples in Microsoft Excel, is also included on the CD.

I hope that this workbook will help users in their learning. Moreover, I hope they find that they can readily apply some of these exercises to problems in their workplaces.

Have a question or feedback? Just send me an e-mail, and I'll be happy to respond. Let me know what works for yc and how we can further improve this workbook. I look forward to hearing from you.

Evan M. Berman
berman@lsu.edu

Q & A

1. Identify five ways in which analysis and data often are used.

The five ways are as follows: (1) to describe and analyze societal problems, (2) to describe policies and programs, (3) to monitor progress and prevent fraud, (4) to improve program operations, and (5) to evaluate policy and program outcomes.

2. How does quantitative analysis assist in decision making?

Quantitative analysis provides a factual underpinning of situations and responses by quantifying the extent of problems and situations and the actual or likely impact of proposed strategies. At the very least, a focus on facts and objective analysis can reduce judgment errors stemming from overly impressionistic or subjective perceptions that are factually incorrect.

3. Identify six competencies for analysis.

The six competencies are as follows: (1) being familiar with data sources in your line of work, (2) being able to collect your own data, (3) analyzing data, (4) communicating results from analysis, (5) bringing to quantitative analysis the theory and practice of management and policy analysis, and (6) having a strong sense of ethics relating to quantitative analysis.

4. What is scientific research?

Scientific research is the careful, systematic process of inquiry that leads to the discovery or interpretation of facts, behaviors, and theories. Scientific research is distinguished from personal and other forms of research or inquiry by rather strict standards for accepting new facts and theories as knowledge and by a process that includes other scientists in making such determinations.

5. What is statistics?

Statistics is the body of systematic knowledge and practice that provides standards and procedures for analyzing one's data. Statistics includes specific tools for analyzing data, too.

6. Identify four stages of proficiency in quantitative analysis.

The four stages of proficiency are as follows: know nothing, journeyman, technocrat, and sophisticated expert. Each stage is associated with distinct development objectives.

7. What three areas of ethical concern are identified in connection with analysis?

The three areas are as follows: (1) fully disclosing the purposes of analysis, (2) integrity in analysis and communication, and (3) concern for the impact of analysis and research on the welfare of human subjects.

8. What is the specific problem of dual purposes?

Analysts must balance potentially conflicting purposes of (1) furthering programs and policies and (2) establishing objective truths about how well a program is performing.

9. *Which practices are associated with furthering the integrity of analysis and communication?*

Analysts should be honest, objective, accurate, and complete. Analysts should not hide facts, change data, falsify results, or consider only data that support a favored conclusion. Analysts should also fully report the sources of their data, data collection methodologies, any possible gaps and shortfalls, and they should assess the impact of such shortcomings on their findings. Results should be presented in straightforward and nonmisleading ways. These norms provide essential guidance to analysts throughout the entire analytical process.

10. *What concern should analysts have for the impact of research on the welfare of human subjects?*

Researchers and analysts should recognize and minimize the potential harm of their research and analysis to research subjects. Most human subject research is now subject to oversight by institutional review boards to ensure that risks to subjects are reasonable and that possible harm is identified and minimized.

CRITICAL THINKING

Note to students: These questions further understanding of selected, key points made in the textbook. Questions in the next section, "Application Exercises," are designed to encourage application of the key points in practice.

1. What is the difference between describing the extent of a social problem and describing the factors that give rise to it? Give an example. How can the latter be useful for developing programs and policies?

   _____

   _____

   _____

   _____

   _____

   _____

2. What is the role of statistics in connection with the six competencies mentioned in the text? What else might be needed to attain these competencies?

   _____

   _____

   _____

   _____

   _____

   _____

3. Many programs produce routine, administrative data that are used to monitor progress and prevent fraud. How useful are such data for the five common uses of analysis and data mentioned in the text? What other data might be needed, such as might be obtained from citizen or client surveys?

   _____

   _____

   _____

   _____

   _____

   _____

4. **Identify a person or situation associated with each of the four stages of proficiency in quantitative analysis.**

_____

_____

_____

_____

_____

_____

5. **Explain how the following concerns of ethics can affect research and its utilization: (1) dual purposes, (2) full disclosure, (3) truthfulness, (4) alternative explanations, (5) communication, and (6) well-being of human subjects. Give examples of each.**

_____

_____

_____

_____

_____

_____

APPLICATION EXERCISES

Note to students: This section is called "Data-Based Exercises" in later chapters (starting in Chapter 6) and will provide you with hands-on exercises that involve real datasets.

1. **Identify five problems or challenges in your area of interest that would benefit from analysis or research.**

_____

_____

_____

_____

_____

2. **Identify at least two examples, in your area of interest, of each of the five common uses of analysis and data.**

_____

_____

_____

_____

_____

3. **What data exist in your area of interest? Are there any datasets with which managers and analysts are expected to be familiar?**

_____

_____

_____

_____

_____

4. At what stage of proficiency do you see yourself? What is necessary to get beyond this stage? Develop some learning objectives for yourself.

_____

_____

_____

_____

_____

5. Explain how a customer or citizen survey might be useful in your area of interest. What topics might such a survey address? What challenges do you foresee?

_____

_____

_____

_____

_____

6. Consider the following proposition: "Almost every department needs people with analytical skills." Verify this proposition by interviewing managers in your area of interest. Also, research salaries at the U.S. Bureau of Labor, National Industry-Specific Occupational Employment and Wage Estimates, at www.bls.gov/oes/current/oessrci.htm, and compare wages for occupations that vary in analytical content, for example, management positions in budgeting, information technology, human resource management, and parks and recreation.

_____

_____

_____

_____

_____

7. Identify and consider some ethical situations that would challenge the integrity of your analysis and research, such as being asked to withhold relevant information. How might you deal with such situations?

_____

_____

_____

_____

_____

8. Research the policies and practices that pertain to ethics in research in your agency or in an agency in your area of interest. If there are none, suggest two or three that would serve as a foundation for a more extensive set of policies.

_____

_____

_____

_____

FURTHER READING

Various books offer additional information about the importance and uses of research and analysis in public service. A classic text about the use of analysis is Aaron Wildavsky, *Speaking Truth to Power: The Art and Craft of Policy Analysis* (Piscataway, N.J.: Transaction Publishers, 1987). Books on policy analysis support the need for research methods and data analysis, such as Eugene Bardach, *Practical Guide for Policy Analysis: The Eightfold Path to More Effective Problem Solving* (Washington, D.C.: CQ Press, 2004) or William Dunn, *Public Policy Analysis: An Introduction* (New York: Prentice Hall, 2003). A classic book about the ethics of analysis is Darrell Huff, *How to Lie with Statistics* (New York: Norton, 1993). A more recent book on this topic is Joel Best, *More Damned Lies and Statistics: How Numbers Confuse Public Issues* (Berkeley: University of California Press, 2004). You can also research the U.S. National Institutes of Health Web site for their latest educational material discussing protections for human subjects. See, for example, www.fic.nih.gov/butrum/H_Subjects/6a.pdf.

In addition, scholarly research can be found on the utilization of research and analysis in agencies, for example, R. Landry, M. Lamari, and N. Amara, "The Extent and Determinants of the Utilization of University Research in Government Agencies" *Public Administration Review* 63 (March/April 2003): 192–205. This article received the Louis Brownlow Award from the American Society for Public Administration for the best article published in *Public Administration Review* in 2003. Scholarship about the use of policy analysis and research in this area traces back to the development of policy analysis as a field in the 1970s and efforts to get public agencies to use it in the 1970s and 1980s. The article by Landry and colleagues has a useful bibliography that reflects the development of this knowledge. Another good bibliographic resource can be found at kuuc.chair.ulaval.ca/english/master.php?url=ressource3.php (Laval University, knowledge transfer and innovation).

As the use of policy analysis and research has become commonplace, scholarly research now emphasizes the ability of agencies to engage in new research efforts or management practices that involve research methods and data analysis. One such effort is performance measurement, and an example of scholarship about the use of analysis in this area is E. Berman and X. Wang, "Performance Measurement in U.S. Counties: Capacity for Reform" *Public Administration Review* 60 (September/October 2000): 409–420. Other scholarly research examines skills that managers need, and the role of analytical and quantitative methods, for example, W. David Patton and Connie Pratt, "Assessing the Training Needs of High-Potential Managers" *Public Personnel Management* 31 (winter 2002), 465–485. Research these sources using your library's databases, such as EBSCOhost, JSTOR, or the like.

Note to students: This chapter includes questions and exercises relating to the textbook introduction to Section II (Research Methods), indicated by SI (Section Introduction).

Q & A

1. What is research methodology? (SI)

Research methodology is the science of methods for investigating phenomena. Research methods are used in almost every social science discipline and can be applied to many different kinds of problems, including those found in public and nonprofit management and analysis.

2. What is basic research? What is applied research? (SI)

Basic research is a research activity whose purpose is to develop new knowledge about phenomena such as problems, events, programs or policies, and their relationships. Applied research is a research activity whose purpose is to develop knowledge for addressing practical problems.

3. What are quantitative research methods? What are qualitative research methods? (SI)

Quantitative research methods involve the collection of data that can be analyzed using statistical methods. The purpose of quantitative research is to quantify the magnitude of phenomena, to provide statistical evidence about factors affecting these phenomena, and quantify the impacts of programs and policies. Qualitative research methods involve the collection and analysis of words, symbols, or artifacts that are largely nonstatistical in nature. Typically the purpose of qualitative research is to identify and describe new phenomena and their relationships.

4. What are variables?

Variables are empirically observable phenomena that vary.

5. What are attributes?

Attributes are the specific characteristics of a variable, that is, the specific ways in which a variable can vary. All variables have attributes. For example, the variable "gender" has two attributes: male and female.

6. How is descriptive analysis different from the study of relationships?

Descriptive analysis provides information about (the level of) individual variables, whereas the study of relationships provides information about the relationships among variables.

7. Define the terms independent variable and dependent variable.

All causal relationships have independent and dependent variables. The dependent variable is the variable that is affected (caused) by one or more independent variables. Independent variables are variables that cause an effect on other variables but are not themselves shaped by other variables.

8. What is a causal relationship, and how is it different from an association?

Most studies describe relationships among variables. When relationships are causal, one variable is said to be the cause of another. When variables are only associated with each other, no effort is made to identify patterns of causation.

9. What is required for establishing a claim of causality?

To establish causality, there must be both empirical correlation and a plausible theory that explains how these variables are causally related.

10. What is a hypothesis?

A hypothesis is a relationship that has not yet been tested empirically.

11. What six steps are involved in program evaluation?

The six steps are as follows: (1) defining program goals and activities, (2) identifying which key relationships will be studied, (3) determining what type of research design will be used, (4) defining and measuring study concepts, (5) collecting and analyzing program data, and (6) presenting study findings.

12. What are rival hypotheses? What are control variables?

Rival hypotheses state threats to the credibility of study conclusions. Control variables are variables used in empirical research to evaluate rival hypotheses.

13. Explain the role of statistics in determining the impact of rival hypotheses (or control variables) on program outcomes.

The impact of rival hypotheses can seldom be ascertained through research design alone. Statistics, then, are used to examine these impacts. (Statistics are also used for other purposes, explained in subsequent chapters of *Essential Statistics for Public Managers and Policy Analysts*.)

14. How are quasi-experimental designs different from classic, randomized experiments?

In a classic experimental design, participants are randomly assigned to either a control or an experimental group. The *only* systematic difference between the groups is that study group participants receive an intervention (called a stimulus, such as a therapy, subsidy, or training). Any outcome differences between these two groups are then attributed to the systematic difference—the treatment. Such testing conditions are seldom possible in public management and policy. Quasi-experimental designs are imperfect research designs that may lack baselines, comparison groups, or randomization that are present in classic, random experiments.

15. What are threats to external validity?

Threats to external validity are those that jeopardize the generalizability of study conclusions to other situations. These threats often concern unique features of the study population or research design.

16. What are threats to internal validity?

Threats to internal validity are those that jeopardize study conclusions about whether an intervention in fact caused a difference in the study population. These threats often question the logic of study conclusions.

CRITICAL THINKING

1. Give examples of basic and applied research questions that might be raised in the context of (1) a program to reduce adult illiteracy and (2) a program that fights international terrorism. (SI)

_____

_____

_____

_____

_____

_____

2. Why are both quantitative and qualitative methods indispensable in addressing questions of basic and applied research? (SI)

_____

_____

_____

_____

_____

_____

3. Give some examples of variables. Why are variables key to research?

_____

_____

_____

_____

_____

_____

4. A program aims to reduce adult illiteracy by providing reading sessions during evening hours. Identify the dependent and independent variables.

dep. var. = illiterate Adults
ind. var = reading sessions Attendance

_____

_____

_____

5. A study examines the impact of gender and drug use on school performance and political orientations. Identify the dependent and independent variables.

_____

_____

_____

_____

_____

_____

6. It is said that in Sweden an empirical association exists between the presence of storks and the incidence of new babies. Explain what is necessary to establish a claim of causation. Do storks really bring babies?

_____

_____

_____

_____

_____

_____

7. A study examines the relationship between race and crime. Is this a causal relationship or an association? Explain.

_____

_____

_____

_____

_____

_____

8. Apply the following statement to program evaluation: "Research begins with asking questions." Think about a program that you know about as a basis for answering this question.

_____

_____

_____

_____

_____

_____

9. The developers of the adult literacy program mentioned in question 4 claim that the program is effective. By what measures might this effectiveness be demonstrated?

_____

_____

_____

_____

_____

_____

10. What might be some rival hypotheses regarding the effectiveness of this adult literacy program?

_____

_____

_____

_____

11. Discuss an experimental research design for testing the effectiveness of an anger management program. Then apply the three quasi-experimental designs mentioned in Box 2.1 in the text.

_____

_____

_____

_____

_____

_____

APPLICATION EXERCISES

1. Give examples of basic and applied research questions in your area of interest. (SI)

_____

_____

_____

_____

_____

2. Give examples of quantitative and qualitative research methods in your area of interest. (SI)

_____

_____

_____

_____

_____

3. Consider the following variables: the number of immigrants, attitudes towards abortion, and environmental pollution. What might be some attributes of each of the variables?

_____

_____

_____

_____

_____

4. You have been asked to develop a neighborhood crime control program. Thinking ahead, you develop a strategy for evaluating the program in subsequent months and years. Define the program and identify dependent and independent variables that can be used to evaluate it.

_____

_____

_____

_____

5. Identify a problem in your area of interest. Identify the dependent and one or more independent variables affecting this problem.

_____

_____

_____

_____

_____

6. Consider a program or policy in your area of interest. How do the specific issues raised in the text regarding program evaluation apply to your program or policy? For instance, give some examples of how difficult it can be to document program outcomes.

_____

_____

_____

_____

_____

7. Discuss how you can apply the six steps of program evaluation to a specific program in your area of interest.

_____

_____

_____

_____

_____

8. Find an article that discusses a specific program evaluation and identify in it each of the six steps of program evaluation.

_____

_____

_____

_____

_____

9. Identify some rival hypotheses (control variables) that might affect conclusions about the effectiveness of an adult literacy program. Then, discuss how an experimental research design and several quasi-experimental designs might be helpful for determining the effectiveness of the program.

_____

_____

_____

_____

10. **Define the objectives of a job-training program, and then identify some rival hypotheses regarding possible outcomes. Explain how baselines and comparison groups might be used.**

_____

_____

_____

_____

_____

FURTHER READING

The all-time, best-selling, easy-to-read general textbook on **research methods** in social science (general) is Earl Babbie, *The Practice of Social Research,* 10th ed. or later (Belmont, Calif.: Wadsworth, 2003). For readers interested in **program evaluation**, the leading text is Peter Rossi et al., *Evaluation: A Systematic Approach,* 7th ed. or later (Thousand Oaks, Calif.: Sage, 2003).

A book that combines program evaluation with performance measurement (see Chapter 4) is James C. McDavid and Laura R. L. Hawthorn, *Program Evaluation and Performance Measurement: An Introduction to Practice* (Thousand Oaks, Calif.: Sage, 2005). For a light version, with practical examples, try Daniel Krause, *Effective Program Evaluation: An Introduction* (Chicago: Nelson Hall, 1996). Some books focus on program evaluation for specific areas, such as schools, criminal justice, and health. A good source with applications in public administration is Joseph Wholey et al., eds., *Handbook of Practical Program Evaluation* (San Francisco: Jossey Bass, 2004). A somewhat more recent source is Gerald Miller and Marcia Whicker, *Handbook of Research Methods in Public Administration* (New York: Marcel Dekker, 1999). This book is somewhat technical and has many chapters about quantitative methods.

Research methods are widely used in scholarly research, of course. The *Journal of Policy Analysis and Management* publishes many articles in which specific programs and policies are evaluated. Some of these articles are grounded in economic thought, though not all. Also, most empirical articles in the leading journals in public administration, political science, and nonprofit management use the terminology of independent, dependent, and control variables discussed in this chapter. You should have no problem picking up any leading, scholarly journal in your field and finding these terms used. A few studies in public and nonprofit management and policy analysis use comparison groups and quasi-experimental designs, but most rely on statistical techniques to account for control variables. These techniques are discussed later in the textbook.

CHAPTER 3

Q & A

1. What is a scale?

A scale is the collection of attributes that is used to measure a specific variable. Scales are important because they define the nature of information about variables.

2. What is a nominal-level scale? What is an ordinal-level scale?

A nominal-level scale exhibits no ordering among the categories. The variable "region" is an example of a variable with a nominal scale. An ordinal-level scale exhibits order among categories, though without exact distances between successive categories. Likert scales are examples of ordinal scales. Variables with ordinal- or nominal-level scales are called categorical (or discrete) variables.

3. What is an interval-level scale? What is a ratio-level scale?

Interval- and ratio-level scales exhibit both order and distance among categories. The only difference between interval and ratio scales is that the latter have a true zero. Income is an example of a ratio-level variable when it is measured in actual dollars; someone who earns $75,000 per year makes exactly three times that of someone making $25,000, and it is possible to make $0 (no income). The distinction between ratio- and interval-level variables is typically of little relevance to public and nonprofit administration and policy analysis. Variables with interval- and ratio-level scales are also called continuous variables.

4. What are incomplete, ambiguous, and overlapping scales? Why must they be avoided?

An incomplete scale omits response categories, an ambiguous scale has ill-defined response categories, and an overlapping scale has at least one response that is covered by more than one category. Incomplete, ambiguous, and overlapping scales should be avoided because they have limited measurement validity.

5. Define and contrast the terms variable and concept.

Variables are empirically observable phenomena that vary, whereas concepts are abstract ideas. Variables are directly observed; concepts are observed indirectly (through variables).

6. Describe the two steps involved in concept measurement.

Concept measurement involves two steps: first, the process of specifying all relevant dimensions of concepts (conceptualization) and, second, the process of specifying which variables will be used to measure (operationalization). Complex concepts and those that are key to the research design are usually conceptualized with greater rigor than are those that are simple or less key to the program or evaluation.

7. What three strategies of operationalization are mentioned in the text?

Three approaches to operationalization are (1) to develop separate measures for each dimension, (2) to develop a single set of measures that encompass the dimensions, or (3) to develop a single measure. These three strategies reflect a declining order of rigor.

8. *What is the theorem of the interchangeability of indicators, and why is it important?*

The theorem of the interchangeability of indicators states that if several measures are equally valid indicators of a concept, then any subset of these measures will be valid as well. In other words, there are many valid ways to measure a given concept. This theorem is important because it implies that the analyst's task is to choose one approach and then justify that that approach is a valid one.

9. *What is an index variable?*

An index variable is a variable that combines the values of other variables into a single indicator or score. Index variables are commonly used to empirically measure abstract concepts and multifaceted phenomena.

10. *How are index variables constructed?*

Index variables are constructed by summing the values of variables that measure distinct, though related, aspects of the concept. When a value of one or more measurement variable(s) is missing, the respective value of the index variable is also missing. (See Table 3.2 in the textbook for an example.)

11. *Name four strategies for validating index variables.*

First, analysts argue that their measurement variables are reasonable from a theoretical perspective (i.e., have content validity). Second, they show that, empirically, index measures have an appropriate range of values. Third, they show that the variables are correlated with each other (that is, they have high internal reliability). Fourth, index variables can be compared with other known measures, derived from external (other studies) or internal (the same study) sources. Respectively, these are referred to as criterion and construct validity.

12. *What is Cronbach alpha? What values are acceptable?*

Cronbach alpha, also called measure alpha, is a measure of internal reliability. This is the extent to which measurement variables are correlated with each other. Variables that measure the same concept are assumed to correlate with each other. Alpha values between 0.80 and 1.00 are considered good, values between 0.70 and 0.80 are acceptable, and values below 0.70 are poor and indicate a need for analysts to consider a different mix of measurement variables that measure their concept.

CRITICAL THINKING

1. Explain the following statement: "Scales should encompass all of the possible values that a variable can assume."

_____

_____

_____

_____

_____

_____

2. Explain the following statement. "Continuous-level scales are preferred over ordinal-level scales, which in turn are preferred over nominal-level scales."

_____

_____

_____

_____

_____

3. Explain how measurement scales (for example, Likert scales) can affect the phrasing of survey questions.

    _____
    _____
    _____
    _____
    _____
    _____
    _____

4. The text states that "no correct number of dimensions or variables exist, only bad or lacking ones." Explain this statement.

    _____
    _____
    _____
    _____
    _____
    _____
    _____

5. The text distinguishes three approaches to operationalization. When should the most rigorous approach be used? When should the least rigorous approach be used?

    _____
    _____
    _____
    _____
    _____
    _____
    _____

6. A study wishes to measure "citizen trust in government" through the number of lawsuits filed against the federal government. Evaluate the measurement validity of this approach.

    _____
    _____
    _____
    _____
    _____
    _____
    _____

7. Explain the theorem of the interchangeability of indicators.

    _____
    _____
    _____
    _____
    _____

8. Explain the following statement: "When one or more of the measurement variables are missing from an observation, the value of the index variables for that observation is missing, too." Also, what are the pros and cons of guessing the values of missing observations? Why should this not be done?

_____

_____

_____

_____

_____

_____

9. Explain the following concepts, and give an example of each: (1) face validity, (2) construct validity, (3) criterion validity, and (4) content validity.

_____

_____

_____

_____

_____

_____

10. Explain the following statement: "Analysts usually collect a few more variables than are minimally needed because they cannot know, prior to reliability analysis, which variable mix will have a sufficiently high alpha score to lend empirical support for the index measure."

_____

_____

_____

_____

_____

_____

APPLICATION EXERCISES

1. Examine the citizen survey in the documentation for the Public Perceptions dataset, in Chapter 18 of this workbook. What level of measurement scale is used for the different items?

I. Likert scale, II. Likert scale, III Likert scale, IV Likert
scale, V. Likert, VI Likert scale, VII Nominal, continuous

_____

_____

2. Give some examples of nominal-, ordinal-, interval-, and ratio-level variables in your area of interest.

Nominal - gender (male/female)
ordinal - educational level (highest degree) (highest to lowest/lowest to highest)
Interval - years of service
(ratio-level
(continuous) number of years on job (giving specific #)

3. An analyst wishes to measure public support for a new welfare program. (1) Develop some suitable measures using Likert items on a survey. (2) Show how incomplete, ambiguous, and overlapping scales create problems of measurement validity.

4. A survey of citizens assesses the extent to which they perceive the federal government works democratically. A second study measures the extent to which the governments of different countries are democratic. Conceptualize *democracy* in each of these two study contexts.

5. Develop an index variable to measure "fear of statistics" among students in pubic and nonprofit management. Then develop an index variable to measure a concept in your area of interest.

    ~~Variable~~ Variable is amount of math class held enough for This class – strongly disagree to strongly agree
    con be's worry if I can succeed in statistics class – strongly disagree to strongly agree
    Do I have enough time to study for this class to succeed – strongly disagree to strongly agree
    ex: each question range is 1-5, add all up of average them (determined by chart choice)
    can use either – Avg is preferred

6. Select a sample of six Government Accountability Office reports (see Box 2.2 in the text) or scholarly articles that use empirical data. Examine how these reports or articles address the matter of measurement validity.

7. Develop some measures that might be used in a study that assesses a neighborhood crime control program. Discuss some challenges of measurement validity, as well as strategies for dealing with these challenges.

FURTHER READING

Conceptualization and measurement are typically discussed in books on research methods and program evaluation, and readers are referred to those mentioned in Chapter 2 of this workbook.

It is instructive to consider articles that show different approaches to operationalizing study concepts. An example of the first approach to operationalization discussed in the text (measures of different dimensions combined in separate indices and subsequently aggregated into a "super" index) is E. Berman and J. West, "What Is Managerial Mediocrity? (Part 1)" *Public Performance and Management Review* 27 (December 2003): 9–29. In this article, the three dimensions of mediocrity are shown in Table 3 (p. 20) and are later combined in an aggregate index. An article that shows the second, less elaborate approach to operationalization (measures of different dimensions combined in a single index) is E. Berman, "Dealing With Cynical Citizens" *Public Administration Review* 57 (March/April 1997): 105–113. In this article, Table 1 shows the items that make up the index of citizen cynicism, and the article also shows triangulation and other strategies of validation. Examples of the third approach are ubiquitous, as they often are used as control variables in research. The above articles include several examples of this approach, as well. You may want to research your library's databases for articles in your area of interest.

CHAPTER

4

Q & A

1. What is performance measurement?

Performance measurement provides a real-time assessment of what a program is doing, what resources it is using, and what it has accomplished recently. As an analytical process, it is designed to produce such information on an ongoing basis; it provides a snapshot that integrates important, frequently quantitative information about programs and policies. Performance measurement helps managers improve program monitoring and accountability, and, by focusing on measurable results, improve program performance and stakeholder satisfaction, too.

2. How is performance measurement related to program evaluation?

Whereas program evaluation focuses on the past (what has a program or policy achieved?), performance measurement focuses on the present (what is a program or policy achieving?). Performance measurement developed from program evaluation. While thorough, program evaluation can be quite cumbersome and hence may produce information that is neither ongoing nor timely for management purposes. By contrast, performance measurement aims to be an up-to-date management information system.

3. What is the logic model?

The logic model is a way of conceptualizing program performance that shows relationships among inputs, activities, outputs, outcomes, and goals. (See the textbook for a schematic model.)

4. What is the difference between outputs and outcomes?

Outputs are the immediate, direct results of program activities. Outcomes are specific changes in behaviors or conditions that are measures of goal attainment.

5. What problem of measurement validity is mentioned in the text in connection with performance measurement, and how is it addressed?

Performance measures should avoid problems of inaccurate or incomplete measurement. In practice, performance measures do have these problems, and managers need to be clear about what their performance measures include and what they do not. Performance measures are best regarded as indicators only, to be used in conjunction with other, often qualitative information about programs and policies.

6. What is effectiveness?

Effectiveness is the level of results of a program or treatment. It is typically measured by one or more output or outcome measures.

7. What is efficiency?

Efficiency is the unit cost to produce a good or service. It is calculated as the output or outcomes over inputs, or O/I. Efficiency indicators can be calculated in different ways and should reflect program management concerns.

8. *What are workload ratios?*

Workload ratios are the ratios of activities over inputs, or A/I. For example, a workload ratio is the number of students in anger management courses per teacher providing such courses. Distinguishing between workload ratios and efficiency measures is important: a high caseload of clients does not mean that they are being served well.

9. *What are benchmarks?*

Benchmarks are standards against which performance is measured. Internal benchmarks are standards that organizations select based on what their own prior programs have achieved, or on what they feel is appropriate. External benchmarks are standards that are set based on the performance of other organizations and programs.

10. *What are equity measures?*

Equity measures are used to compare performance across different groups. Often, outputs and outcomes measures can be analyzed for different populations, types of organizations, and the like.

11. *What is forecasting? How is it related to planning?*

A forecast is a prediction about the future. This is sometimes also called a projection or prognosis. Forecasting is different from planning; whereas forecasting discusses what the future will look like, planning provides a normative model of what the future should look like. Planning often starts with forecasting to establish what the future is likely to look, in order to develop alternative futures or scenarios that might be preferred.

12. *How are statistical methods used for forecasting?*

Statistical methods typically describe and aim to extrapolate quantitative trends based on past and present data. Analysis can involve no more than the simple extrapolation of the past few data points, but it can also analyze complex cyclical patterns and model other variables affecting past and present levels.

13. *What are judgment-based methods of forecasting?*

Judgment-based methods of forecasting often use experts to assess the likelihood of futures occurring. Experts can be brought together in groups, or as individuals. For example, the Delphi method is a forecasting method that asks experts to respond anonymously through several rounds of written surveys.

14. *What are some key practices and standards for making forecasts?*

Forecasts are more reliable for shorter periods; forecasting should use multiple methods; data and experts should be as up-to-date and valid as possible; forecasts should use as much information as possible about the past, present, and future; assumptions and limitations should be clearly stated; the accuracy of forecasts should be determined wherever possible; forecasts of more complex methods are not always more accurate than simple ones; forecasting should begin by identifying a full range of possible future scenarios and events; forecasting should note unusual past events that affect past data, and adjust forecasts or the data accordingly; forecasters should expect their forecasts to be challenged.

CRITICAL THINKING

1. How is a system of key indicators such as performance measurement different from a system of comprehensive measurement?

    _____

    _____

    _____

    _____

2. Explain how performance measurement provides useful information about programs and policies, even if it is not free from measurement errors.

_____

_____

_____

_____

_____

3. Is the number of arrests by police officers an activity, an output, or an outcome? Explain your answer.

Output - b/c it is the result of the activity

_____

_____

_____

4. Give an example of the distinction between efficiency and a workload ratio not mentioned in the text.

efficiency: ~~output~~ out come over ~~input~~ or output over input

workload: ~~ratio of~~ activity over input

_____

5. Examine the measures in Table 4.1 in the textbook. Can you improve on these? Can you identify other measures? In what way might inaccurate or incomplete data affect these measures?

_____

_____

_____

_____

6. What practical problems can you foresee in using external benchmarks? Can these problems be overcome? If so, how?

_____

_____

_____

_____

_____

7. Explain how equity measures are important, especially in the context of public management.

_____

_____

_____

_____

8. Discuss some challenges to using performance measurement and how you might address them.

_____

_____

_____

_____

_____

_____

9. Explain the following statement: "Experts can help identify future events that trend forecasting may overlook." Give an example.

_____

_____

_____

_____

_____

_____

10. Discuss the following statement: "The accuracy of forecasts should be determined, such as by comparing predictions about the present against the observed reality of the present."

_____

_____

_____

_____

_____

_____

APPLICATION EXERCISES

1. Identify outputs and outcomes of a program to increase high school student graduation rates through homework assistance for at-risk students.

_____

_____

_____

_____

2. Identify outputs and outcomes of a program to reduce traffic congestion by adding dedicated bus lanes (lanes that only buses can use).

outputs - People who ride buss, People who drive
decreased # of Cars
outcomes - decreased travel time, reduced traffic congestion
Overall

3. **Develop a complete performance measurement system for a program or policy in your area of interest. Identify inputs, activities, outputs, outcomes, and goals, as well as measures of effectiveness, efficiency, and equity. See Table 4.1 in the textbook to get you started. You will want to add efficiency, effectiveness, and equity.**

---

4. **Research and compare examples of performance measurement in agencies in your area of interest. How similar are their measures? Can you explain the differences?**

---

5. **Look for examples of performance measurement and balanced scorecards on the Internet.**

---

6. **Identify some statistical forecasts in your area of interest. What assumptions do they make? How might they be improved?**

---

7. **Develop some scenario-based forecasts in your area of interest.**

FURTHER READING

For a practical manual on conducting performance measurement, see Center for Accountability and Performance, *Performance Measurement: Concepts and Techniques,* 3d ed. (Washington, D.C.: American Society for Public Administration, 2004). The classic work is Harry Hatry et al., *How Effective Are Your Community Services? Procedures for Measuring Their Quality* (Washington, D.C.: Urban Institute and International City/County Management Association [ICMA], 1992). See also ICMA, *A Guide to Results-Oriented Government and Performance Measurement* (Washington, D.C.: ICMA, 2004). This guide provides overviews of comparative performance measurement, helping jurisdictions in their benchmarking. Another useful book is David Ammons, *Municipal Benchmarks: Assessing Local Performance and Establishing Community Standards,* 2d ed. (Thousand Oaks, Calif.: Sage Publications, 2001).

Although many books discuss forecasting methods, most of these books are for business, for example, J. Scott Armstrong, *Principles of Forecasting: A Handbook for Researchers and Practitioners* (Norwell, Mass.: Kluwer, 2001). Armstrong also maintains an extensive Web site (www-marketing.wharton.upenn.edu/forecast/), which provides a useful introduction to the field. Many policy analysis books include some chapters on forecasting, such as Dipak K. Gupta, *Analyzing Public Policy: Concepts, Tools, and Techniques* (Washington, D.C.: CQ Press, 2001). Another such book is William Dunn, *Public Policy Analysis: An Introduction* (New York: Prentice Hall, 2003). However, these chapters often provide little more than a very brief overview of the field.

Q & A

1. What are administrative data, and for what purposes are they used?

Administrative data are generated in the course of managing programs and activities. Traditionally, administrative data are used to (1) ensure that resources are not misused, (2) monitor the status of activities, and (3) provide a record of what has been completed and accomplished. Today, administrative data are also collected to (4) meet the needs of performance measurement. These purposes may also be necessary for grant or contract compliance.

2. What are secondary data, and for what purposes are they used?

Secondary data are data that have been collected by other agencies for their own purposes but that are available to managers and may be relevant for their purposes. Secondary data can provide important information about communities and can be useful for needs assessment, benchmarking, and outcome measurement. Managers and analysts are expected to be familiar with the secondary data in their fields.

3. What types of surveys are mentioned in the text, and for what purposes are surveys used?

The three types of surveys are mail, phone, and in-person surveys. Surveys are commonly used in program evaluation research and, increasingly, performance measurement. Surveys are increasingly used when such knowledge needs to be quantitative, comprehensive, and systematic.

4. Discuss the pros and cons of different types of surveys. Why are phone surveys used increasingly?

Phone surveys have important speed advantages but may have low response rates. In-person surveys offer the highest response rate but also the highest cost. Mail surveys allow for the most survey items, but the need for follow-up mailings increases the duration of data collection. Phone surveys are used increasingly because they can be completed in a short time and can be used to ask many questions.

5. List some standards for writing survey questions.

Survey questions should be clear (unambiguous and specific) and easy to answer. They should avoid double-barreled and leading questions. And they should avoid negative statements.

6. Explain the limitations and uses of customer comment cards.

Customer comment cards generate samples that are typically not representative of all customers, and therefore, they are not generalizable. They are useful, however, for obtaining feedback about problems that might need attention.

7. Which sources of data, other than administrative records and surveys, are mentioned in the text?

The chapter mentions trained observers, actors, experts, and focus groups.

8. What is a census?

A census is a survey or count (tally) of an entire group or population.

9. ***Why is obtaining a representative sample important? How is it different from a purposive sample?***

Only representative samples allow for generalization to the population. Representative samples have a mix of characteristics similar to that of the population from which they are drawn, whereas purposive samples have an unrepresentative mix of characteristics (for example, "exemplary practices" surveys are often purposive samples). Some threats to validity for surveys are inadequate sampling frames and unrepresentative samples.

10. ***What is random sampling, and why is it important?***

Random sampling is a sampling method whereby each member of the population has an equal chance of being selected for the sample. Random sampling is the most valid way of making representative samples.

11. ***Define sampling error. Do small or large samples have small sampling errors? Why?***

The sampling error is the percentage by which sample findings vary in 95 of 100 repeated samples. Large samples better reflect population characteristics and thus have smaller sampling errors.

12. ***What is nonresponse bias?***

Nonresponse bias occurs when the views of nonrespondents are different from those of respondents, thus affecting the generalizability of the sample.

CRITICAL THINKING

1. Identify some examples of the use of administrative data.

2. Identify and discuss the problems in the quality of administrative data.

3. Identify some examples of the use of secondary data.

4. Identify and discuss the problems in the quality of secondary data.

_____

_____

_____

_____

_____

5. Contrast the use of systematic surveys and focus groups. For which purposes is each best suited? Give some examples.

_____

_____

_____

_____

_____

6. Consider the following statement: "Our city is larger than the city next door, so we need a larger sample size for doing our citizen survey." Is this statement valid? Why, or why not?

_____

_____

_____

_____

_____

7. Discuss the following statement: "Over 50 items can be asked when questions (in phone surveys) are easy and asked in a similar format." Find an example on the CD that accompanies the text.

_____

_____

_____

_____

_____

8. Explain the concept of sampling error and why it matters.

_____

_____

_____

_____

_____

9. What practical problems do you see with drawing a random sample of all Americans as opposed to a random sample of those that live in your city?

_____

_____

_____

_____

10. Discuss why customer comment cards do not constitute a generalizable customer satisfaction survey.

_____

_____

_____

_____

_____

11. Identify threats to validity arising from biased questions and sampling in surveys.

_____

_____

_____

_____

_____

APPLICATION EXERCISES

1. Identify administrative data in your field of interest. How can such data be used for managing programs?

_____

_____

_____

_____

_____

_____

2. Critique the validity of administrative data in your field of interest. How might the quality of administrative data be improved?

_____

_____

_____

_____

_____

_____

3. Identify secondary data in your field of interest. For what purposes might these be used?

_____

_____

_____

_____

_____

4. Discuss how trained observers, actors, experts, and focus groups might be used in your field of interest.

    _____

    _____

    _____

    _____

    _____

5. Identify how client and citizen surveys might be used in your field of interest.

    _____

    _____

    _____

    _____

    _____

6. Use the Internet to find examples of client and citizen surveys in your field of interest. Then evaluate the (1) validity and (2) usefulness of these surveys.

    _____

    _____

    _____

    _____

    _____

7. Evaluate and improve the following survey question: "Please tell me whether you like living at your present location or would consider moving to another city."

    _____

    _____

    _____

    _____

    _____

8. Develop some other poor survey questions, and then improve them. Use a Likert scale (see Chapter 3).

    _____

    _____

    _____

    _____

    _____

9. Develop a survey of clients, citizens, or employees in your field of interest.

    _____

    _____

    _____

    _____

10. **Examine the methods section in the survey report on the CD that accompanies the book. Examine carefully how concerns about representative samples are dealt with.**

_____

_____

_____

_____

_____

_____

FURTHER READING

The leading text on survey research is Don Dillman, *Mail and Internet Surveys: The Total Design Method,* 2d ed. (New York: Wiley, 1999). For conducting citizen surveys for administrative purposes, see Thomas Miller and Michele Miller, *Citizen Surveys: How to Do Them, How to Use Them, What They Mean,* 2d ed. (Washington, D.C.: International City/County Management Association, 2000). A book on public opinion polling from a political perspective is Herbert Asher, *Polling and the Public: What Every Citizen Should Know,* 6th ed. (Washington, D.C.: CQ Press, 2004). A book on focus groups is Richard Krueger and Mary Casey, *Focus Groups,* 3d ed. (Thousand Oaks, Calif.: Sage, 2000). A good book on secondary data sources is Mark Maier, *The Data Game,* 3d ed. (Armonk, N.Y.: M. E. Sharpe, 1999). Despite the publication date, this book contains authoritative discussions about the quality of secondary data in different fields of interest, such as demography, housing, health, education, crime, the economy, labor, and business. These chapters are essential reading for anyone dealing with secondary data in these specific fields.

CHAPTER 6

Note to students: This chapter includes questions and exercises relating to the textbook introduction to Section III (Descriptive Statistics), indicated by SI (Section Introduction).

Q & A

1.   What are descriptive statistics? Give some examples. (SI)

Descriptive statistics provide summary information about variables, such as their average and frequency distribution.

2.   What is the distinction between univariate and bivariate analysis? (SI)

Univariate analysis describes single variables, whereas bivariate analysis examines the relationship between two variables.

3.   What are some important tasks of analysts engaged in statistics? (SI)

Some important tasks of analysts engaged in statistics are as follows: (1) understanding the definition and purpose of a statistic, (2) ensuring that a statistic is appropriate to the data and problem at hand, (3) understanding the test assumptions of a statistic, (4) applying a statistic to the problem at hand in ways that are mindful of the preceding points, (5) drawing correct conclusions, and (6) communicating results in ways that are appropriate for both professional and general audiences.

4.   Explain data coding, data input, and data cleaning. (SI)

Data coding is the process of preparing data (from pen-and-paper surveys or electronic or other sources) for input into statistical software programs. Data input (also, data entry) is the activity of recording these data in statistical software programs. Data cleaning is the process of identifying and removing reporting and recording errors. Errors include mistyped values, errors that arise in the process of uploading, and other implausible values that have been recorded. It is common practice to assume that unexamined data usually contain various errors that must be identified and removed.

5.   What are variables? What are scales? (review)

Variables are succinctly defined as empirically observable phenomena that vary (see Chapter 2 in the text). Scales are the collection of specific attributes (or values) used to measure a specific variable (see Chapter 3 in the text). There are four levels of measurement scales: nominal, ordinal, interval, and ratio. You need to be familiar with these concepts, as they are key to choosing the correct statistic.

6.   What role does the measurement level play in univariate analysis?

The type of univariate statistics that should be used depends on the level of measurement.

7.   Name the three measures of central tendency. How is each defined?

The three measures of central tendency are mean, median, and mode. The mean is the sum of a series of observations, divided by the number of observations in the series. The median is the middle value in a series (or array) of values that have been ordered from low to high. The mode is the most frequent (typical) value(s) of a variable.

8. How should analysts deal with the problem of missing data in calculating statistics?

The most common approach is to exclude such observations from calculations.

9. What is a weighted mean? For what purposes is it sometimes used?

The weighted mean is defined as a mean for which the observations have been given variable weights. Weighted means are commonly used to adjust for over- and undersampling in surveys, for example.

10. What is the formula for determining the location of the median?

The location of the median is determined by the formula $(n + 1)/2$. For example, if there are 97 observations, the median is the value of the 49th observation, when observations have been ordered. When there are 98 observations, the median is the mean of the 49th and 50th observations.

11. When should both the mean and median be used? When should the mode be used?

The median should be reported along with the mean when a few very large or very small observations affect the value of the mean. The mode is used infrequently, but an advantage of the mode is that it can be used with nominal-level data, which is not possible for calculating the mean or median.

CRITICAL THINKING

1. Give some examples of univariate and bivariate analyses. (SI)

_____

_____

_____

_____

_____

2. Explain the following statement: "It is common practice to assume that unexamined data usually contain various errors." Give some examples. (SI)

_____

_____

_____

_____

_____

3. Identify four specific ways in which data that have not been thoroughly cleaned may be problematic. (SI)

_____

_____

_____

_____

_____

4. Why is the mean frequently used?

_____

_____

_____

_____

_____

5. Consider the following statement: "Calculating the mean is straightforward, but managers and analysts may encounter some practical issues that, for the most part, concern the data rather than the formula itself." Give examples of these practical issues.

_____

_____

_____

_____

_____

_____

6. Why are observations with missing values typically removed before calculating specific statistics?

missing values means there may be flaws in survey
questions

_____

_____

_____

7. Discuss the challenge of using the mean for calculating the central tendency of an ordinal-level variable (for example, a survey question that uses a Likert scale; see Box 3.1 in the text).

_____

_____

_____

_____

_____

_____

8. Explain the following statement: "The median should always be used when a few very large or very small values affect estimates of the mean." Give some examples of variables for which the median is typically used.

_____

_____

_____

_____

_____

_____

9. Explain the following statement: "An advantage of the mode is that it can be used with nominal-level data, which is not possible for calculating the mean or median."

_____

_____

_____

_____

_____

DATA-BASED EXERCISES

1. Although computer software is used to calculate statistics, some students find that hand calculation furthers their conceptual understanding. Consider the following values: 4, 5, 7, 9, 11, 13, 13, 16, 18. Calculate the mean, median, and mode. After completing the exercise below, you might return to your results and verify them using the computer. (To practice, you can make up your own data, too.)

Mean: $\sum x_i/n =$ _____

Median: Value of observation at location $(n+1)/2$: _____

Mode: Most frequent value: _____

2. This is an exercise in data input. Data input is a skill that is specific to the software package you are using. Chapter 17 provides data input examples for SPSS. Input the data shown in the workbook Screen W17.4, and use SPSS to calculate the mean, median, and mode. Verify your results with those shown in Screen W17.8.

3. This is an exercise in data coding and input. Input the data from Table W6.1 into your statistical software program. For simplicity, the table shows only three respondent records of the three survey items. Note that respondent number 3 did not answer the first question. This needs to be coded as missing. Code this value as a "9" and instruct your statistical software to treat this value as missing. Also, create variable and value labels, as shown in Screens W17.3 and W17.4.

Table W6.1 ——— Selected Data from Three Survey Respondents

How important are the following issues for you? Please state whether you consider each issue Very Important, Important, Somewhat Important, or Unimportant:

Respondent 1:

	Very Important	Important	Somewhat Important	Unimportant
Controlling government spending	[ ]	[x]	[ ]	[ ]
Cutting property taxes	[x]	[ ]	[ ]	[ ]
Reducing I-4 congestion	[ ]	[x]	[ ]	[ ]

Respondent 2:

	Very Important	Important	Somewhat Important	Unimportant
Controlling government spending	[ ]	[x]	[ ]	[ ]
Cutting property taxes	[ ]	[ ]	[ ]	[x]
Reducing I-4 congestion	[x]	[ ]	[ ]	[ ]

Respondent 3:

	Very Important	Important	Somewhat Important	Unimportant
Controlling government spending	[ ]	[ ]	[ ]	[ ]
Cutting property taxes	[x]	[ ]	[ ]	[ ]
Reducing I-4 congestion	[x]	[ ]	[ ]	[ ]

4. Read about the Community Indicators dataset in Chapter 18 of the workbook. Then open this dataset using your statistical software package (for example, SPSS). Compare the mean and median

values of the number of murders ("Murder") in these different cities. Are the values of the mean and median similar or dissimilar? Calculate the mean and median of other variables of your choice, too. In Chapter 7, we will take this analysis further by making frequency distributions.

_____

_____

_____

_____

_____

_____

5. Using the Community Indicators dataset, calculate the mean burglary rate per capita. To do this, you first need to create a new variable, which is the burglary rate per capita for each city in the dataset. Let's call this variable "burglaryrate" and define it as burglary/pop, whereby "burglary" and "pop" correspond to the variable names on the Community Indicators dataset. Use your statistical software program to calculate the mean and median burglary rate per capita. Which three cities have the highest burglary rates per capita? Are these the same cities as those with the largest number of burglaries?

_____

_____

_____

_____

_____

_____

_____

Note for students using SPSS: See Screen W17.26. Type "burglaryrate" (without quotes) in the target variable field, and type "burglary/pop" (without quotes) in the numeric expression field. Select OK and see the new variable created in your Data Editor screen. It will have been added at the end of the existing variables, all the way to the right in the Data View screen, or at the end of the list in the Variable View screen. You may want to change the number of decimals shown to, say, five (5); see Screen W17.3 for this purpose.

6. Open the Watershed dataset and read the description of this survey in workbook Chapter 18. Calculate the mean and median of the number of samples that exceed pollution standards (Conpolut) and fish and wildlife advisories (Advisory).

_____

_____

_____

_____

7. *Optional* (see appendix to Chapter 6 in the text): Consider the table of grouped data (Table W6.2). Calculate the grouped mean and grouped median.

Table W6.2 ————〜〰〜—— Frequency Table

Category	Interval of variable "x"	Frequency	Cumulative frequency
1	1–4	33	33
2	5–8	47	80
3	8–11	64	144
4	12–15	32	176
5	16–19	14	190

Grouped Mean
Step 1: Calculate the weighted mean of categories:

_____

_____

_____

Step 2: Calculate the estimated value of the variable mean:

_____

_____

_____

Grouped Median
Step 1: Determine the location of the median:

_____

_____

_____

Step 2: Calculate the estimated value of the variable median:

_____

_____

_____

Note: Chapter 7 contains more introductory data-based exercises, such as involving frequency charts and frequency distributions. Many analyses, including exercises in data cleaning, involve the techniques discussed in that chapter.

FURTHER READING

The statistics described in this chapter are quite basic. A fun, introductory book to statistics is Larry Gonick and Woollcott Smith, *The Cartoon Guide to Statistics* (New York: HarperPerennial, 1993). It does a nice job of explaining statistical concepts and includes many of the statistics described in subsequent chapters. Somewhat less useful is Murray Spiegel and Larry Stephens, *Schaum's Outlines: Statistics,* 3d ed. (New York: McGraw-Hill, 1999). It has chapters on descriptive statistics and other statistics discussed in this course, but the treatment is not very applied. Of course, you can consult many basic books on statistics, but few focus on public affairs. For example, R. Mark Sirkin, *Statistics for the Social Sciences,* 3d ed. (Thousand Oaks, Calif.: Pine Forge Press, 2005) is written in an accessible style, and it emphasizes learning through understanding and application of mathematical calculations. Another option is Chava Frankfort-Nachmias and Anna Leon-Guerrero, *Social Statistics for a Diverse Society,* 4th ed. (Thousand Oaks, Calif.: Sage, 2005). The suggested readings in Chapter 2 related to the ethics of data analysis and presentation also provide useful advice on basic statistics, for example, Darrell Huff, *How to Lie with Statistics* (New York: Norton, 1993).

A good exercise on the road toward mastering concepts and applications in statistics is to view their use in scholarly research and professional practice. For example, read some issues of leading academic journals and note their use of descriptive statistics. Some of the leading journals in public affairs and political science are *American Political Science Review, Public Administration Review,* and *Journal of Public Policy Analysis and Management.* Of course, many good scholarly journals are available, and you might ask your professor for a reading list or even for specific articles highlighting the uses of statistics discussed in this and subsequent chapters.

If you are using SPSS and you want more information than is offered in Chapter 17 of this workbook, try the most recent version of *SPSS Base User's Guide* (Chicago: SPSS) for whatever version of SPSS you are using. Or you can call SPSS Inc., at 312-651-3000. You can also try Earl Babbie and Fred Halley, *Adventures in Social Research: Data Analysis Using SPSS 11.0/11.5 for Windows* (Thousand Oaks, Calif.: Pine Forge Press, 2003), or later editions, as available. Even though the Babbie and Halley book is based on an earlier version of SPSS, it should help if you are looking for additional assistance with SPSS.

Q & A

1. What are measures of dispersion?

Measures of dispersion provide information about how the values of a variable are distributed.

2. What are frequency distributions? What are they used for?

Frequency distributions describe the range and frequency of values of a variable. They are used for nominal- and ordinal-level data. Frequency distributions often are a prelude for generating data tables and attractive graphics and are also used for data cleaning.

3. What is a histogram? How is it different from a bar chart?

A histogram shows the number of observations in different categories (or values) of the variable. Analysts can define the number (or widths) of categories that are used to group the different values of the variable. Bar charts are similar, but they show the number of observations for each different value of the variable. By convention, histograms are used for continuous variables, and bar charts are used for categorical variables.

4. Discuss the use of bar charts, pie charts, and line graphs.

Bar charts show the frequency of occurrences through stacks, which can be used to highlight the importance of categories (values). Bar charts are used with ordinal- or nominal-level variables. Pie charts typically are used to focus on equality: Who gets most (or least) of what? Pie charts are used with nominal-level variables. Line graphs are usually used for continuous variables, partly to avoid displaying a large number of bars.

5. What is a boxplot? For what purpose is it used?

A boxplot is a graphical device that shows various measures of dispersion. Boxplots are useful for obtaining a quick, visual, preliminary understanding of data; they are useful tools for data cleaning. Statistics associated with boxplots are calculated based on the location of data.

6. What is the midspread? The inner fence?

Both terms are associated with boxplots. The midspread (also called interquartile range, or IQR) is defined as the difference between the third and first quartiles. The inner fence is an imaginary point that lies 1.5 times the IQR below the first quartile. Values below this point are called outliers, as are data points with values greater than the outer fence (which is defined as an imaginary point that lies 1.5 times the IQR above the third quartile).

7. What is an outlier? How are they dealt with?

Outliers are analyst-defined observations with unusual values relative to other values in the data. Outliers are defined as observations whose values are either less than the inner fence or greater than the outer fence. Outliers may be the result of data-coding errors or reflect actual but unusual values in the sample. The textbook suggests that observations that are flagged as outliers generally should be retained when they are not coding errors, when they are plausible values of the variable in question, and when they do not greatly affect the value of the mean (of continuous variables).

8. What is the standard deviation?

The standard deviation is a measure of dispersion that is calculated based on the values of the data.

9. What statistical property makes the standard deviation a desirable statistic?

When data are normally distributed, 68.3 percent of the observations lie within ±1 standard deviation from the mean, 95.4 percent lie ±2 standard deviations from the mean, and 99.7 percent lie ±3 standard deviations from the mean.

10. How do analysts determine whether a variable is normally distributed?

Some analysts rely on a visual inspection, aided by a computer-generated curve that is superimposed over the histogram. Analysts also use measures of skewness and kurtosis to determine whether the shape of the observed curve is consistent with a normal distribution. Sample data are not expected to match a theoretical bell-shaped curve perfectly because of deviations due to chance selection.

11. What are standardized variables?

Standardized variables (also called z-scores) are variables that have been transformed such that their means are exactly 0 and their standard deviations are exactly 1 (or unity).

CRITICAL THINKING

1. Explain how frequency distributions assist with data cleaning.

    _____
    _____
    _____
    _____
    _____

2. When variables are continuous, analysts will have to transform their variables, grouping values into categories, before making a frequency distribution. Explain and give an example.

    _____
    _____
    _____
    _____
    _____

3. Explain the following statement: "When recoding variables or creating histograms, a practical question is how wide each category should be. To avoid perceptions of lying with statistics, a rule of thumb is that categories should be based on category ranges of equal length."

    _____
    _____
    _____
    _____

4. **Describe the difference between a histogram, a bar chart, and a stem-and-leaf plot.**

_____

_____

_____

_____

5. **What is the purpose of boxplots, and why are they uncommon in final reports?**

_____

_____

_____

_____

6. **Is a quartile a range of values or a unique value?**

_____

_____

_____

_____

7. **Is a boxplot fence an actual observation or a calculated number? And what about a whisker?**

_____

_____

_____

_____

8. **Research some innovative ways of using graphs to get your points across.**

9. **Using Figure W7.1, draw a boxplot of a variable with these values: 4, 5, 7, 9, 11, 13, 13, 16, 18, and 24. Are there any outliers? Why, or why not?**

Figure W7.1 ———————∿∿∿—Application: Boxplot

10. **What percentage of observations has a higher z-score value than 0.86? What percentage of observations has a lower z-score value than –1.15? What useful questions can a z-score statistic help answer?** *Hint:* **In the normal distribution table (see Appendix A in the textbook), look up values of the absolute difference between the above z-score values and 0.50 (|0.5 – z-score|).**

_____

_____

_____

_____

DATA-BASED EXERCISES

1. Although the computer calculates statistics, some students find that hand calculation furthers their conceptual understanding. Consider the following values: 4, 5, 7, 9, 11, 13, 13, 16, 18. (These were also used in workbook Chapter 6, Data-Based Exercise 1.) Now, calculate the IQR, inner fence, outer fence, and standard deviation. You can use the computer to verify your results.

IQR: First quartile: _____

Third quartile: _____

IQR (third quartile – first quartile): _____

Inner fence: First quartile – (1.5*IQR): _____

Outer fence: Third quartile + (1.5*IQR): _____

Standard deviation: $\sqrt{\dfrac{\sum(x_i-\bar{x})^2}{n-1}}$

$\bar{x}$: _____

$x_1 - \bar{x}$: _____ $(x_1 - \bar{x})^2$: _____

$x_2 - \bar{x}$: _____ $(x_2 - \bar{x})^2$: _____

$x_3 - \bar{x}$: _____ $(x_3 - \bar{x})^2$: _____

$x_4 - \bar{x}$: _____ $(x_4 - \bar{x})^2$: _____

$x_5 - \bar{x}$: _____ $(x_5 - \bar{x})^2$: _____

$x_6 - \bar{x}$: _____ $(x_6 - \bar{x})^2$: _____

$x_7 - \bar{x}$: _____ $(x_7 - \bar{x})^2$: _____

$x_8 - \bar{x}$: _____ $(x_8 - \bar{x})^2$: _____

$x_9 - \bar{x}$: _____ $(x_9 - \bar{x})^2$: _____

$\sum(x_i - \bar{x})^2$: _____

$\sqrt{\dfrac{\sum(x_i-\bar{x})^2}{n-1}}$: _____

2. This is an exercise in data cleaning. Prior to performing any type of data evaluation, you must first become familiar with the dataset and the nature of the variables you wish to evaluate. The first dataset is from a citizen survey performed in Orange County, Florida. Open the Public Perceptions dataset.

a. Read the description of this dataset, the methodology, the survey instrument, and notes regarding the variables and values.

b. How many observations are contained within this dataset? _____

c. How many variables are contained in the set? _____

d. What are the measurement levels of the variables Gender, Age, and Yearsorc? Yearsorc measures the number of years that the respondent has lived in Orange County. Determining measurement levels is relevant to the selection of statistics later. The measurement level can be determined in many ways, for example, by making a frequency chart and examining the category values.

Gender: _____

Age: _____

Yearsorc: _____

e. We will now examine whether the present variable values are plausible (that is, whether they make sense). Make a frequency distribution for the variable Yearsorc. Are these values plausible?

_____

f. To further validate your suspicions, make a boxplot of the variable Yearsorc. What do you conclude?

_____

_____

g. Let's remove this observation. It is quite unlikely that someone has actually lived 301 years in Orange County. It might be a coding error (or a practical joke), but in any event we are unable to obtain the correct value at this point. Note also that the revised boxplot still indicates some outliers. However, these are quite plausible values. We use our judgment and decide to retain them.

h. Run some boxplots on other variables. Do you need to make any other changes?

_____

3. **According to the Public Perceptions survey, do residents feel that the county has done a good job of balancing growth with environmental concerns? Make a frequency distribution. The variable is named Balance. Also, construct two bar charts: one that includes all three categories, and one that omits the category "don't know."**

_____

_____

_____

_____

_____

4. **According to the Public Perceptions survey, how do residents feel about their service experience? Specifically, what percentage of respondents agree or strongly agree that employees were helpful? What percentage of respondents agree or strongly agree that service was provided in a timely manner?**

    Note: Analyze data for only those respondents who stated that they have had contact with county employees during the last twelve months.

_____

_____

_____

_____

_____

5. **Among the items listed in section I of the Public Perceptions survey, which five items are the most important? Which items are the least important for residents? Based on what statistic do you decide this? What type of graph might you use to present your findings?**

_____

_____

_____

_____

_____

6. Open the Community Indicators dataset. Examine the frequency distributions of the variables murder and nonnegligent manslaughter (called "Murder" on the dataset), burglary (called "Burglary"), and forcible rape (called "Rape"). Then use boxplots to determine whether any cities might be considered outliers among these measures. Based on your findings, should you include or exclude these cities from any further analysis? If you include them, should you note and study the impact that these cities have on your results?

_____

_____

_____

_____

_____

7. The Employee Attitudes survey contains several items that reasonably might affect workplace performance. Read the description of this survey. How do employees feel about the following items: the morale among county employees, the extent that their organization welcomes change, receiving timely feedback about performance, and cooperation among departments? The variables are, respectively, Himorale, Welchang, Feedback, and Coopdept.

_____

_____

_____

_____

_____

8. Open the Watershed dataset and read the description of the survey. Calculate the mean and median of the number of samples that exceed pollution standards (Conpolut) and fish and wildlife advisories (Advisory). Make a bar chart of the quality of watersheds (Wshedch).

_____

_____

_____

_____

_____

From Data Coding to Data Analysis

Below is a checklist of items for getting your data in order.

1. Does the dataset include all of the observations (for example, respondents)?

2. Does the dataset include all of the variables?

3. Has a sample of the dataset been compared against the actual observations for accuracy?

4. Do the variable names make sense?

5. Does each variable have a label (if needed)?

6. Does each variable value have a label (if needed)?

7. Have variable values that indicate a missing value been coded as missing?

8. Has each variable been checked for implausible values (including outliers)?

9. Have implausible values been corrected or omitted?

10. Do the ranges of variables make sense? Which variables have limited ranges, and what implications follow for subsequent analysis?

FURTHER READING

The readings discussed in Chapter 6 should help with the material here, too. Basic statistics books will discuss standard deviations, bar charts, and the like. Another useful book is Mark Berenson et al., *Basic Business Statistics,* 3d ed. (Upper Saddle River, N.J.: Pearson Education, 2005).

Few separate articles or books deal with data cleaning. On the Internet, visit paul.rutgers.edu/~weiz/readinglist.html. Some books on data mining, which deals with getting information from large databases, discuss the importance of data cleaning. Some scholarly articles draw attention to problems with data, though these books often are quite sophisticated. In the end, the message is clear: we need to get our data in shape by trying to detect errors.

Graphical displays are increasingly used in presentations, of course. This may be a good time to familiarize yourself with standards of making presentations (for example, with PowerPoint) and the use of graphics. See, for example, Cliff Atkinson, *Beyond Bullet Points* (Redmond, Wash.: Microsoft Press, 2005). In addition, you might want to visit a Web site like www.smartdraw.com to become familiar with graphics and other visual representations.

CHAPTER
8

Q & A

1. What are bivariate statistics? How do bivariate analyses help managers and policymakers?

Bivariate statistics is the study of relationships among two variables. Providing empirical information about relationships is a key step in determining program effectiveness, and bivariate statistics can help managers and policymakers by determining how variables affect key outcomes.

2. What is a contingency table?

A contingency table expresses the relationship between two categorical variables. One variable is shown in rows and the other in columns. The cells show the number (and, often, percentages) of observations associated with specific values of the two categorical variables.

3. How does causality affect the design of contingency tables?

When bivariate relationships between two categorical variables are causal, the independent variable should be placed in the columns and the dependent variable in the rows. When relationships are associations, there is no preference concerning the placement of variables. Although this convention often is violated, following it makes the analysis of tables easier when column percentages are used, as is commonly the case.

4. How are column percentages calculated? How are they used for examining relationships?

Column percentages are calculated by dividing each frequency by the column total. Relationships in contingency tables are usually examined by comparing column percentages across (groups of) rows.

5. What are marginal totals?

Marginal totals are the row and column totals.

6. What is a statistical definition of a relationship?

A statistical relationship means that as one variable changes, so too, does another.

7. What is a positive relationship? What is a negative relationship?

Relationships involving ordinal or continuous variables are characterized as positive or negative. A positive relationship means that large values of one variable are associated with large values of the other variable and that small values of one variable are associated with small values of the other variable. A negative relationship implies the opposite: large values of one variable are associated with small values of the other variable, and vice versa.

8. What is a pivot table? How is it different from a contingency table?

Pivot tables show statistics of one or more continuous variables for one or more categorical variables in the data cells. By contrast, the cells of contingency tables show the number (and, often, percentages) of observations associated with specific values of the two categorical variables.

9. *What is a layer variable?*

A layer variable is one that defines the subset of data used for subsequent data tables.

10. *What does the term* transposing *mean?*

Transposing means interchanging the column and row variables; column variables become row variables, and vice versa.

CRITICAL THINKING

1. Identify all of the features that are part of contingency tables: title, clear column and row headings, data cell frequencies, column percentages, marginal totals, and grand total.

_____

_____

_____

_____

_____

2. Explain the following statement: "Examining relationships in contingency tables is usually based on comparing column percentages for each or groups of rows." Give an example.

_____

_____

_____

_____

_____

3. Calculate column percentages for Table W8.1:

Table W8.1 ———— ᴧᴧ— Welfare Outcomes by Level of Education

	Education		
Welfare outcome	No H.S. degree	H.S. degree	Some college
Low	60	55	10
Medium	35	55	15
High	25	30	20

Note: H.S. = high school.

4. Practice writing up the results for the preceding question. Identify the number of recipients and how they differ by education and welfare outcome. Then discuss the relationships between these two variables. Use statements in the form of "Whereas *xx* percent of recipients with no high school degree have high welfare outcomes, *xx* percent of recipients with some college have high welfare outcomes," and so on.

_____

_____

_____

_____

_____

5. Explain how pivot tables and contingency tables are relevant to analysis of problems in your area of interest. Provide some examples.

_____

_____

_____

_____

_____

6. Study the latest issues of research journals or professional reports in your field of interest; examine the use of tables and how the reports are written up. Record your findings on a separate sheet.

DATA-BASED EXERCISES

Note to students: The following exercises are designed to give you practice making contingency tables and pivot tables. However, because the interpretation of contingency tables is often difficult without the use of the statistics presented in Chapter 9, some of the write-up and interpretation regarding these tables is postponed until the next chapter.

1. Use the Employee Attitudes dataset. Examine the relationship between gender and the morale of county employees (Himorale). Then consider the relationship between gender and stress (Stressed). Use column percentages, and write up the results.

_____

_____

_____

_____

_____

_____

2. Use the Public Perceptions dataset. Consider the relationship between gender (Gender) and trusting the county government to do what is right most of the time (Trust). Is the difference between men and women large or small? Is it meaningful to describe the relationship as being positive or negative?

_____

_____

_____

_____

_____

3. Use the Public Perceptions dataset. The three most important issues are (see part I of the survey in Chapter 18): helping public schools (Pubschl), fighting illegal drug use (Figtdrug), and dealing with the problems of gangs (Gangs). Do whites and nonwhites agree on the importance of these priorities? On which issues is there a difference?

_____

_____

_____

_____

_____

4. Use the Employee Attitudes dataset. A manager wishes to examine the relationship between race (Race) and perceptions that the people who get promoted are among the best qualified (Bestqual) in the Public Works Department. However, very few employees are minorities, and a manager is concerned that separate analysis for each minority group might reveal their identity. Therefore, the manager wants to compare Caucasian employees against non-Caucasian employees. Recode the variable Race in this manner, and report on the above relationship.

_____

_____

_____

_____

_____

_____

5. Use the Employee Attitudes dataset. Examine the relationship between the morale of county employees (Himorale) and being satisfied with one's job (Satisjob). Is this table easy or difficult to interpret? *Note:* The statistics discussed next, in Chapter 9, help to interpret whether a relationship exists between these two variables and, if so, whether it is positive or negative.

_____

_____

_____

_____

_____

_____

6. Open the Watershed dataset, and make a pivot table from variables in that dataset. For example, consider region and drinking water impairment as the two categorical variables, and show the mean level of conventional pollutants in each data cell. You may choose other continuous variables, as well. *Note:* See footnotes 6 and 8 in Chapter 8 of the textbook for information on how to create pivot tables in SPSS and Excel.

_____

_____

_____

_____

_____

_____

FURTHER READING

This chapter deals with contingency tables and pivot tables. Although no specialized texts cover these matters, user's manuals and published articles provide further reading. For example, *SPSS 14.0 Base User's Guide* (Upper Saddle River, N.J.: Prentice Hall, 2005 or later editions), has separate chapters on using contingency tables (called Crosstabs in SPSS) and pivot tables. Otherwise, many articles and reports show the use of contingency tables, and students can examine how these authors interpret and write up the results. One such article, discussed in Chapter 3, is E. Berman, "Dealing With Cynical Citizens," *Public Administration Review* (March/April 1997): 105–113. In this article, Table 3 is a contingency table. You can also visit the Government Accountability Office (GAO) Web site for examples of reports with tables. One such report, which includes results from a survey of state agencies, is GAO, *Mad Cow Disease: FDA's Management of the Feed Ban Has Improved, but Oversight Weaknesses Continue to Limit Program Effectiveness* (Washington, D.C.: U.S. Government Printing Office, 2005), appendix 4 (p. 47), www.gao.gov/new.items/d05101.pdf.

CHAPTER 9

Q & A

Note to students: This chapter includes questions and exercises relating to the textbook introduction to Section IV (Inferential Statistics), indicated SI (Section Introduction).

1. What are inferential statistics? (SI)

Inferential statistics are statistics used to make inferences about characteristics in the population from which sample data were drawn. Most commonly, inferential statistics are used to determine, on the basis of a sample, whether a relationship exists in the population from which the sample data were drawn.

2. Name three types of bivariate tests. Explain when each should be used. (SI)

There are many statistical tests for bivariate data. The type of data (level of measurement) determines which statistical test should be used. The section introduction discusses the following:

• When two variables are categorical, tests based on contingency tables should be used.

• When one variable is dichotomous (for example, gender) and the other is continuous, the t-test should be used.

• When both variables are continuous, simple regression analysis should be used.

3. Which five steps are followed in deciding the statistical significance of relationships?

1. State the null hypothesis (in Greek letters).

2. Choose a statistical test (see the introduction to Chapter 9 in the textbook).

3. Calculate the test statistic (t.s.), and evaluate test assumptions.

4. Look up the critical value (c.v.) of the test.

5. Draw conclusion:

   If | t.s. | < c.v., do not reject null hypothesis.

   If | t.s. | ≥ c.v., reject the null hypothesis.

4. Explain the purpose of stating the null hypothesis.

The purpose of stating the null hypothesis is to establish a reasonable ground that a relationship exists. By assuming that a relationship doesn't exist, we need only to find a reasonable ground that it does exist, which is that it should be very unlikely to find a test statistic (in the sample) of a given (large) magnitude when in fact no relationship exists in the population. If we assume that a relationship does exist, we might be guilty of not trying hard enough to prove that it doesn't exist.

5. Discuss why notations in hypotheses are usually stated in Greek letters instead of Roman letters.

Greek letters are used because hypotheses refer to relationships in the general population, not in the specific sample.

6. What is the value of chi-square when two variables are unrelated to each other? What happens to the chi-square value as variables are more closely related to each other?

When two variables are (perfectly) unrelated to each other, the value of chi-square is (exactly) zero. The value of chi-square increases as two variables are more related to each other.

7. Define chi-square mathematically. Explain the concepts of "observed" and "expected" frequencies.

Chi-square is defined as $\sum_i \dfrac{(O_i - E_i)^2}{E_i}$, where O_i is the observed frequency in a cell and E_i is the expected frequency in a cell. Observed frequencies are the actual counts of observations in cells. Expected frequencies are cell counts that are expected when no relationship exists between the variables.

8. What are the three test assumptions that must be satisfied in order to ensure that the chi-square test is valid?

First, the variables must be categorical. Second, the observations must be independent. Third, cells must have a minimum of five expected observations. (When the latter is not the case, it is usually because the contingency table contains a large number of rows and columns relative to the number of observations. That is, the data are spread too thinly across too many cells. To correct this problem, adjacent rows or columns are combined to create a smaller number of cells.)

9. Explain the concept of statistical significance.

The concept of statistical significance relates to the following question: "On repeated sampling, *how often* would I be wrong to conclude that a relationship exists when in fact it doesn't exist?" The statistical standard in the social sciences is 5 percent; that is, we are willing to tolerate a 1-in-20 chance of concluding that the null hypothesis should be rejected, when in fact it shouldn't. Standards of 1-in-100 (1 percent) are also used.

10. What is a critical value? Which two parameters determine it?

The critical value is the minimum value of a test statistic that is used to reject the null hypothesis. The critical value of any test statistic is determined by (1) the desired level of statistical significance and (2) the number of degrees of freedom (df).

11. What are the rules for determining whether a relationship is statistically significant?

We compare the absolute value of the test statistic against the critical value of the test statistic at a given level of significance. When the absolute value of the test statistic is greater than or equal to the critical value, we conclude that a relationship exists at the given level of significance. By convention, we report that relationships are not significant, significant at the 5 percent level, or significant at the 1 percent level. *Note:* Statistical software programs calculate the test statistic and report the level of statistical significance at which the test statistic is significant.

12. Explain how the sample size affects the level of statistical significance.

Relationships are more likely to be statistically significant when working with large datasets than when dealing with small ones. This reflects that having more information increases our confidence in our conclusions. The sample size affects the magnitude of many widely used test statistics, including chi-square.

13. What is the practical relevance of relationships? How is this different from statistical significance?

Hypothesis testing merely establishes whether a relationship is present. If present, managers and analysts will want to describe it further in order to determine its importance for management action and public policy. This is called practical relevance (or practical significance). After the statistical significance of relations has been determined, analysts should ask: (1) What is the *direction* of the relationship, specifically, is it a positive or negative relationship? (2) By *how much* does one variable increase or decrease as a result of changes in the other? and (3) What is the *strength* of the relationship?

14. ***Discuss the strategy for evaluating rival hypotheses in contingency table analysis. Also, define the terms*** explanation, replication, specification, *and* suppression.

The strategy for evaluating rival hypotheses in contingency table analysis involves taking control variables into account. The textbook provides an example of this methodology. Explanation is what occurs when statistically significant bivariate relationships are explained away (cease to exist) after adding the control variable. Replication is what occurs when statistically significant bivariate relationships remain significant after adding the control variable. Specification is what occurs when some statistically significant bivariate relationships are explained away after adding the control variable. Suppression is what occurs when a statistically insignificant bivariate relationship becomes significant after adding the control variable. Suppression is rare.

CRITICAL THINKING

1. Why does it make sense to test for relationships by stating the null hypothesis?

    _____

    _____

    _____

    _____

    _____

2. Why are standards of 1 percent and 5 percent often used? What objections might be raised against using standards of, say, .01 percent or 10 percent?

    _____

    _____

    _____

    _____

    _____

3. Explain why the null hypothesis is rejected when the test value exceeds or is equal to the critical value.

    _____

    _____

    _____

    _____

    _____

4. Distinguish between statistical significance and practical relevance. Can you find some examples in your area of interest where a statistically significant result might be practically irrelevant?

    _____

    _____

    _____

    _____

    _____

5. Why must all cells in a chi-square test have a minimum of five expected observations? (See footnote 6 in Chapter 9 of the textbook.)

    _____

    _____

    _____

    _____

    _____

6. What is the critical value for a chi-square test with 13 degrees of freedom at the 1 percent level of significance? If the chi-square test statistic were 16.98, what would you conclude regarding the null hypothesis? What would you conclude if the chi-square value were 68.03?

    Critical value:

    _____

    _____

    Conclusion if chi-square is 16.98:

    _____

    _____

    Conclusion if chi-square is 68.03:

    _____

    _____

7. A statistical software program reports a test to be significant at "p = .035." At what level of significance should this be reported by the analyst (that is, 1 percent or 5 percent)? And what about "p = .056," "p = .0000," and "p = .9989"?

    p = .035:

    _____

    _____

    p = .056:

    _____

    _____

    p = .0000:

    _____

    _____

    p = .9989:

    _____

    _____

8. Formulate three null hypotheses in a study that examines the impact of community-based policing on neighborhood crime.

    Null hypothesis 1:

    _____

    _____

    _____

Null hypothesis 2:

_____

_____

_____

Null hypothesis 3:

_____

_____

_____

9. Use Table W9.1 to design a contingency table of overall health and the number of days worked (Table W9.1). Think up the data. Identify the dependent variable, and be careful where you place it in the table. Show both percentages and frequencies.

Table W9.1 ——————⟿— Application: Table

10. Calculate chi-square for the hypothetical data shown in Table W9.2, and determine whether the relationship is statistically significant. Welfare outcomes (for example, time to find a job) are examined as a function of the education levels of welfare recipients. Use Table W9.3 to calculate your expected frequencies. Use Table W9.4 to calculate the chi-square values for each cell.

Table W9.2 ——————⟿— Welfare Outcomes by Level of Education

	Education		
Welfare outcome	No H.S. degree	H.S. degree	Some college
Low	60	55	10
Medium	35	55	15
High	25	30	20

Note: H.S. = high school.

Table W9.3 ——————⟿— Application: Welfare Outcomes by Level of Education, Expected Frequencies

	Education			
Welfare outcome	No H.S. degree	H.S. degree	Some college	Total
Low				
Medium				
High				
Total				

Note: H.S. = high school.

Table W9.4 ———~~~~ Application: Welfare Outcomes by Level of
Education, Chi-Square Values

	Education			
Welfare outcome	No H.S. degree	H.S. degree	Some college	Total
Low				
Medium				
High				
Total				

Note: H.S. = high school.

11. **Examine Table W9.5. Does this contingency table satisfy the test assumptions for chi-square? Why or why not? If not, what might be done to correct the problem?**

Table W9.5 ———~~~~ Welfare Outcomes by Level of Education
(Table W9.2 revised)

	Education			
Welfare outcome	No H.S. degree	H.S. degree	Some college	Total
Low	5	9	3	17
Medium	7	8	2	17
High	1	2	0	3
Total	13	19	5	37

Note: H.S. = high school.

12. **Good writing starts with knowing what to write—an outline or list of topics. Assume that you are an analyst with the National Institutes of Health, and your data show a statistically significant relationship between exercise and the risk of heart disease. Identify five things that you will want to report on in the "Results" section of your report. Consider statistical as well as practical significance. List any charts or visual aids you will use.**

1. _____

2. _____

3. _____

4. _____

5. _____

DATA-BASED EXERCISES

Note: Some of these exercises draw on those first presented in Chapter 8.

1. **Use the Employee Attitudes dataset. Examine the relationship between stress (Stressed) and the morale of county employees (Himorale). Note the measurement scale of the variables. What do you conclude? Do you consider this a causal relationship or an association? Does the analysis satisfy the assumptions of the chi-square test? If not, what categories might you combine to overcome this problem?**

_____
_____
_____
_____
_____
_____

2. Use the Public Perceptions dataset. Is the relationship between watching Orange TV (Watch), the county's cable television station, and trusting the county government to do what is right most of the time (Trust) statistically significant? Do you consider this a causal relationship or an association? Does the analysis satisfy the assumptions of the chi-square test? If not, how might you address this problem?

    _____

    _____

    _____

    _____

    _____

    _____

3. Use the Public Perceptions dataset. Examine the relationship between residents who trust the county government to do what is right most of the time (Trust) and their belief that county government works efficiently (Works). What is the practical significance of this relationship?

    _____

    _____

    _____

    _____

    _____

    _____

4. Use the Public Perceptions dataset. In workbook Chapter 8, Data-Based Exercise 4, you evaluated the importance of selected issues. The three most important issues were helping public schools (Pubschl), fighting illegal drug use (Figtdrug), and dealing with the problems of gangs (Gangs). Do whites and nonwhites agree on the importance of these priorities? On which issues is there a difference? Discuss the practical importance of any significant differences.

    _____

    _____

    _____

    _____

    _____

    _____

5. Use the Employee Attitudes dataset. This is an exercise in examining control variables. First, examine the relationship between gender (Gender) and the perceived morale of county employees (Himorale). What do you conclude? Next, test the rival hypothesis that this relationship is spuriously caused by stress: maybe one gender experiences a higher level of stress. (To this end, recode the variable Stressed into two groups: high stress and low stress.) What do you conclude?

    _____

    _____

    _____

    _____

    _____

    _____

6. Examine the variables in the Employee Attitudes dataset. Identify five relationships that you hypothesize to be statistically significant. Test these hypotheses. What do you find?

_____

_____

_____

_____

_____

_____

FURTHER READING

There exists no shortage of "general purpose" introductory statistics texts, and most of them discuss hypothesis testing. If you seek additional assistance on this topic, my recommendation is to peruse your local library shelves until you find a book that you like. Statistics books explain this topic in similar yet subtly different ways. The textbooks suggested here explain hypothesis testing and contingency table analysis in a clear manner. I hope that you like my approach, but feel free to choose whatever works for you. Sometimes, it is just a matter of seeing the same thing from different angles.

Some statistics texts have been mentioned in Chapters 6 and 7, and these will likely help here, too. Sam Kash Kachigan, *Multivariate Statistical Analysis: A Conceptual Introduction,* 2d ed. (New York: Radius Press, 1991) is an inexpensive book that does an exemplary job of explaining advanced statistics concepts in nonmathematical terms, but the coverage of topics is advanced, perhaps aimed at doctoral students. Another option is Tari Renner, *Statistics Unraveled: A Practical Guide to Using Data in Decision Making* (Washington, D.C.: International City/County Management Association, 1988). Of course, you can also compare our treatment with that of another book in public affairs, Kenneth Meyer, Jeffrey Brudney, and John Bohte, *Applied Statistics for Public Administration,* 6th ed. (Florence, Ky.: Thomson Learning, 2006).

CHAPTER 10

Q & A

1. What is proportional reduction in error?

Proportional reduction in error (PRE) is the improvement, expressed as a fraction, in predicting a dependent variable from knowledge of the independent variable. PRE ratios range from 0.00 (no association or improvement in prediction) to 1.00 (perfect association or prediction). Although there are no absolute standards for PRE scores, many analysts regard scores of less than 0.25 as indicating a weak association, scores between 0.25 and 0.50 as moderate association, and scores above 0.50 as strong association.

2. What are paired cases used for? What is the difference between "similar pairs" and "dissimilar pairs"?

Some PRE statistics are calculated based on paired cases. Similar pairs are pairs of observations that have similar rankings on two variables, that is, observations rank similarly low (or high) on both variables. Dissimilar pairs are pairs of observations that have reverse ranking on two variables—one observation scores high and the other low, and vice versa, on both variables. Tied pairs are those that have similar rankings on one variable and dissimilar rankings on the other variable. PRE statistics based on paired cases have a range of –1 to +1, which provides information about both the strength and the direction of relationships. For example, a PRE test statistic based on paired cases with a value of –0.57 indicates a strong, negative relationship between two variables.

3. What does the term dependent samples refer to?

Dependent samples (also called related samples) are those in which the selection of one subject in a sample does affect the selection of subjects in another group. Examples of dependent samples are those that involve before-and-after test scores, subjects that have been matched (or paired) in some way, and evaluators' ratings. Separate statistical tests exist for dependent samples.

4. What is the difference between symmetric and directional measures?

Some PRE measures vary depending on which variable is designated as dependent. Such measures are called directional. By contrast, symmetric measures do not vary according to which variable is designated as dependent.

5. Name four measures of association for two ordinal variables, and compare them.

Four measures of association for two ordinal variables are gamma (γ), Somer's d, Kendall's tau-b (τ_b) and Kendall's tau-c (τ_c). These PRE statistics differ chiefly in the manner in which ties are taken into account. Of these, tau-b often has the smallest PRE value and is widely used.

6. For what purpose is Goodman and Kruskal's tau (τ_{yx}) used?

Goodman and Kruskal's tau is a PRE measure that is used for testing the association of two nominal variables.

7. What is the goodness-of-fit test?

The goodness-of-fit test is used to determine whether an ordinal distribution or test result is consistent with a predetermined norm.

8. For what purpose is the McNemar test used? How does it differ from other tests?

The McNemar test is used for two-by-two tables with paired observations. It is frequently used for testing discrimination. The McNemar test differs from many other tests in that it determines the level at which *dissimilar outcomes* are statistically significant. The McNemar test ignores cases with similar outcomes.

9. What problems are associated with small samples, and how are they addressed by two-by-two tables? What are some tests for small samples?

Tests often fail to reject the null hypothesis when samples are small. Analysts frequently combine categories in order to increase the information in each cell, thus reducing the number of rows and columns. This may result in two-by-two tables. The chi-square with continuity correction and the Fisher exact test are tests for small samples.

10. Which test statistics are used for comparing ratings across programs or program components?

Kruskal-Wallis' H and the Friedman test are often used to compare ratings across programs or program components. Both tests assign ranks to raters' ratings, and then determine the level at which the mean of ranks is different across each of the different programs or program components.

11. How does the Friedman test differ from the Kruskal-Wallis' H test?

Whereas the Kruskal-Wallis' H test assumes independent observations, the Friedman test assumes dependent observations.

CRITICAL THINKING

1. Explain why PRE is a measure of the strength of relationships.

_____

_____

_____

2. Give some examples of dependent and independent samples.

_____

_____

_____

3. In what ways is tau-c a more useful measure than chi-square?

_____

_____

_____

4. You have conducted a citizen survey and want to know whether respondents' assessments about environmental and economic conditions are associated. Both items are measured on a seven-point Likert scale. Which test statistic might you use, and why?

Test statistic and rationale:

_____

_____

_____

5. You are a senior staff member with the Federal Aviation Administration. Flight delays have been a major issue with the public of late, and one of your contractors has proposed a new system that promises to reduce the number of delays that exceed 10 minutes. To test whether the system works, you will implement it at a major airport and measure delays during the late afternoon rush hour. The average delay will be calculated daily for the late afternoon period. Which test statistic can be used to answer the question of whether the new system has reduced average delays that are greater than 10 minutes? For this purpose, use a dichotomous variable that measures, for each day, whether the average delay exceeded 10 minutes. Also, what is the fewest number of days that the airport must implement the system in order to determine (at the 1 percent level of significance) whether the system effectively reduces the average delay to less than 10 minutes?

    Test statistic and rationale:

    _____

    _____

    _____

    Minimum sample size:

    _____

    _____

    _____

6. You are a manager with a state employment agency. In one of your districts, managers have implemented a new program and after six months of trial (and error), it is decided to bring in a panel of outside experts to evaluate it. You would like to have the option to later disregard any evaluator whose assessment sharply disagrees with others. How many experts should you bring in? How many different aspects should they each evaluate? Should they evaluate the same aspects or different aspects? Which statistical test should you use, and how does that affect your answer?

    Number of evaluators and rationale:

    _____

    _____

    _____

    Test statistic and number of items:

    _____

    _____

    _____

7. As a manager, you want to know whether your employees are treating service requests from white and minority program clients in a similar manner. You decide to send pairs of white and minority testers to your agencies with similar service requests. Which test statistic might you use, and why?

    Test statistic and rationale:

    _____

    _____

    _____

8. If you wanted to examine the effects of different job training programs on employment outcomes, which statistical test would you use, and why? (*Note:* Answers vary depending on the level of measurement you choose with regard to these variables.)

Test statistic and rationale:

_____
_____
_____
_____
_____
_____

9. **Identify questions that can be addressed using the following tests: McNemar test, chi-square, and Kendall's tau-c. Identify one question per test.**

   McNemar:

   _____
   _____

   Chi-square:

   _____
   _____

   Kendall's tau-c:

   _____
   _____

DATA-BASED EXERCISES

1. Use the Public Perceptions dataset. Previously, in Chapter 9 of this workbook, we used chi-square to examine the relationship between residents who trust the county government to do what is right most of the time (Trust) and their belief that county government works efficiently (Works). Re-examine this relationship using measures of gamma, Somer's d, Kendall's tau-b, and Kendall's tau-c. What do you conclude?

   _____
   _____
   _____
   _____
   _____

2. Use the Public Perceptions dataset. What is the association between having a positive view of the county government (Posview) and satisfaction with the various services that are mentioned, such as law enforcement (Lawenf)?

   _____
   _____
   _____
   _____
   _____

3. Three interviewers are evaluating five job candidates. After interviews and analysis of qualifications and skills, the interviewers are asked to rank the five job candidates. The rankings shown in Table

W10.1 are obtained (1 = high, 5 = low). Which job candidate has the highest level of approval? Do the raters agree? How do your results change when a fourth evaluator is added with rankings identical to those of the first evaluator?

_____

_____

_____

_____

_____

Table W10.1 ———⟋⟍— Ranking of Job Candidates

	Job candidates				
Interviewer	#1	#2	#3	#4	#5
1	2	1	4	3	5
2	4	2	3	1	5
3	3	2	1	4	5

4. A manager wants to know whether whites and minorities are receiving similar or disparate answers to their inquiries. To this end, 15 pairs of testers are sent with identical questions. Testers report to the study supervisor the answers as received, which are then evaluated as satisfactory or unsatisfactory. The result shown in Table W10.2 is obtained. Do whites and minorities receive different treatment?

_____

_____

_____

_____

_____

Table W10.2 ———⟋⟍— Outcomes by Race

	White		
Minority	Satisfactory	Unsatisfactory	Total
Satisfactory	8	1	9
Unsatisfactory	3	3	6
Total	11	4	15

5. In a sample of 57 students, 35 pass a test. Is this consistent with a norm that states that at least 67 percent of students should pass the test? Is it consistent with a norm of 80 percent? What test statistics should you use?

_____

_____

_____

_____

_____

6. **Examine the Employee Attitudes dataset. Use tau-c to test five associations of your choice. Of those that are statistically significant, which are also practically relevant? Why? Practice writing up your results.**

_____

_____

_____

_____

_____

FURTHER READING

Many basic statistics books have separate chapters on the use of the statistics for categorical variables. Comprehensive treatment of this subject is found in Lawrence L. Giventer, *Statistical Analysis for Public Administration* (Belmont, Calif.: Wadsworth, 1997). This book covers the material presented in this single chapter over multiple chapters, and numerous applications and examples of hand calculations of test formulas are provided. Another solid treatment is found in Ronet Bachman and Raymond Paternoster, *Statistical Methods for Criminology and Criminal Justice* (New York: McGraw-Hill, 2003), chaps. 11 and 16.

CHAPTER

11

Q & A

1. When should a t-test be used?

T-tests are used for testing whether two groups have different means. One variable is dichotomous, whereas the other is continuous.

2. What is the null hypothesis of a t-test?

The null hypothesis of a t-test is that the means of a variable do not differ between two groups in the population; that is, the two means are equal. Rejecting the null hypothesis implies that the two group means are different in the population.

3. Name four t-test assumptions.

(1) One variable is continuous, and the other variable is dichotomous.
(2) The two distributions have equal variances.
(3) Observations are independent.
(4) The two distributions are normally distributed.

4. How do researchers test for the normality of variables?

Researchers typically use a combination of visual inspection and statistical tests, such as the Kolmogorov-Smirnov test, to determine the normality of variables. It is acceptable to consider variables as being normally distributed when they visually appear to be so, even when the null hypothesis of normality is rejected by normality tests. Of course, variables are preferred that are supported by both visual inspection and normality tests.

5. What is the purpose of the Levene's test of the equality of variances?

The purpose of the Levene's test is to test whether groups have equal variances. This test is used to test one of the four t-test assumptions and is always used prior to testing the equality of means.

6. What is a paired t-test?

The paired t-test often is used when using before-and-after measurements, such as when assessing student scores before and after tests. Paired t-tests are used when analysts have a dependent rather than an independent sample.

7. What is a one-sample t-test?

A one-sample t-test is used to test whether the mean of a variable is significantly different from a user-specified value.

8. What is the difference between parametric and nonparametric tests? Which type of test is the t-test?

Parametric tests make assumptions about the distribution of data and also are used to make inferences about population parameters. Formally, the term "parametric" means that a test makes assumptions about the distribution of the underlying population. Parametric tests have more test assumptions than nonparametric tests, and most typically assume that the variable is continuous and normally distributed.

9. **What are the advantages and disadvantages of using nonparametric alternatives to t-tests?**

The chief advantage of nonparametric alternatives is that they do not require that continuous variables be normally distributed. The chief disadvantage of nonparametric alternatives is that they are less likely to reject the null hypothesis. A further, minor disadvantage is that nonparametric alternatives do not provide descriptive information about variable means; separate analysis is required for that.

10. **What is a nonparametric alternative to the independent-samples t-test?**

Nonparametric alternatives to the independent-samples test are the Mann-Whitney (U) and Wilcoxon (W) tests. The Mann-Whitney and Wilcoxon tests are equivalent, and both are simplifications of the more general Kruskal-Wallis' H test, discussed in Chapter 10.

11. **What is a nonparametric alternative to the paired-samples t-test?**

A nonparametric alternative to the paired-samples t-test is the Wilcoxon signed rank test.

12. **What is a nonparametric alternative to the one-sample t-test?**

The Wilcoxon signed rank test can also be adapted as a nonparametric alternative to the one-sample t-test. Then, analysts create a second variable that, for each observation, is the test value.

CRITICAL THINKING

1. Explain the importance of the four test assumptions of the independent-samples t-test.

_____

_____

_____

_____

_____

2. Why is the assumption of equal variances irrelevant for the paired-samples t-test?

_____

_____

_____

_____

_____

3. Explain the following statement regarding tests for normality: "Whereas failure to reject the null hypothesis indicates normal distribution of a variable, rejecting the null hypothesis does not indicate that the variable is not normally distributed."

_____

_____

_____

_____

_____

4. Table W11.1 is the printout of a t-test (independent samples). The continuous variable is an index variable of environmental concern. The dichotomous variable is a measure of education (college

versus no college). Interpret and write up the results. What other information would you like to have about this relationship?

_____

_____

_____

_____

Table W11.1 ⎯⎯⎯ ∿ ⎯ Analysis of Environmental Concerns by Education: T-Test Output

Variable	Levene's test for equality of variances			t	df	p (2–tailed)
	F	p				
Environmental concern	1.065	.304	Equal variances assumed	3.705	118.00	.000
			Equal variances not assumed	3.728	117.92	.000

5. Table W11.2 is the printout of a paired-samples t-test. The data are before-and-after measurements of a public safety program. Interpret and write up the results. What other information would you like to have about this relationship?

_____

_____

_____

_____

_____

Table W11.2 ⎯⎯⎯ ∿ ⎯ Comparing "Before" and "After" Results of a Public Safety Program: Paired T-Test Printout

Pair	Mean	t	df	p (2–tailed)
Before - After	−1.497	7.310	193	.000

6. Table W11.3 shows the result of the Kolmogorov-Smirnov test for a variable and three of its transformations. Which variable(s) should the analysts consider for subsequent use?

_____

_____

_____

_____

Table W11.3 ⎯⎯⎯ ∿ ⎯ Testing for Normality

	Kolmogorov-Smirnov		
	Statistic	df	Significance
Index	0.095	102	0.025
SQRT index	0.304	102	0.200
Log index	0.098	102	0.006
Squared index	0.057	102	0.200

7. You are analyzing your data and, using a boxplot, you see some outliers. Should your initial approach be to remove them or to keep them? Why? What are the pros and cons of each approach?

_____

_____

_____

_____

_____

DATA-BASED EXERCISES

1. Use the Watershed dataset. Replicate the analysis in the text. First, analyze the normality of the variable Conpolut and consider various transformations, as shown in Figures 11.3 and 11.4 of the textbook. Then, replicate the t-test for comparing the East (defined as Northeast and Southeast combined) with all other regions.

_____

_____

_____

_____

_____

2. Use the Watershed dataset. Do states in the East vary in the number of fish and wildlife advisories that have been made? (Use the variable Advisory.) Is the variable Advisory normally distributed? If not, what transformation do you suggest?

_____

_____

_____

_____

_____

3. Use the Public Perceptions dataset. An analyst wants to know whether men and women have different perceptions of customer service. To this end, we will use an index variable of customer satisfaction (see Chapter 3); the index variable is provided on the dataset as the last variable, Satisfac, but you can also practice making this index variable in the following way:

From among those respondents who have had contact with a county employee (that is, if contact = 1), create an index variable of "customer service" that is composed of the six survey items: "employees were helpful," "employees treated me with courtesy and respect," "employees were friendly," "service was provided without mistakes," "the service experience exceeded my expectations," and "service was provided in a timely manner." If you are using SPSS, see Chapter 17 of this workbook for instructions on creating index variables in SPSS.

After you have either created this variable or identified this variable on the dataset, address the question of whether men and women vary in their customer satisfaction experience.

_____

_____

_____

_____

_____

4. Use the Public Perceptions dataset. An analyst wants to know whether the index variable of customer service varies across race. Recode the Ethnic variable to distinguish among whites, blacks, other races, and Hispanics. If you are using SPSS, see Chapter 17 of this workbook for instructions on recoding variables in SPSS.

_____
_____
_____
_____
_____
_____

5. Men and women are asked to rank six issues in the order of priority. See Table W11.4. Do men and women differ in their order of priorities? Which test statistic would you use? Can you think of some other situations that match this scenario?

_____
_____
_____
_____
_____
_____

Table W11.4 ⎯⎯⎯ ∿∿ Rank Ordering of Six Priorities

Men	Women
1	3
2	1
3	2
4	6
5	4
6	5

6. A group of 12 welfare recipients participate in training. Before-and-after abilities are measured through a standardized test. See Table W11.5. Is there evidence of improvement? Compare the results of both the paired-samples t-test and the nonparametric alternative.

_____
_____
_____
_____
_____
_____

Table W11.5 ———— ᴡᴡ— Before-and-After Test Scores

Recipient	Before	After
1	4.5	6.7
2	3.2	4.2
3	5.8	5.2
4	3.9	4.3
5	4.2	4.1
6	3.9	4.8
7	2.6	3.2
8	5.2	4.8
9	4.5	4.5
10	3.9	4.1
11	3.8	3.6
12	4.2	5.9

7. Consider Table 11.5 again. Is the after-test score consistent with a norm of 5.0? And with a norm of 6.0? Use both parametric and nonparametric tests. Compare the results.

_____
_____
_____
_____
_____
_____

FURTHER READING

Most statistics books discuss t-tests, although they vary in their coverage of formulas and test assumptions. An in-depth discussion of t-tests is found in David Howell, *Statistical Methods for Psychology,* 5th ed. (Belmont, Calif.: Wadsworth, Duxbury Press, 2001), chap. 7. The *SPSS User's Guide* (Chicago: SPSS, Inc., 1999 or later editions as available) has excellent examples of the use of t-tests in practice and, in a separate chapter, gives some further examples of variable transformations. Ronet Bachman and Raymond Paternoster, *Statistical Methods for Criminology and Criminal Justice* (New York: McGraw-Hill, 2003), has a good discussion of the central limit theorem (also mentioned in Chapter 10).

12

Q & A

1. For what purpose is simple regression used?

Simple regression is used for testing the relationship between two continuous variables, whereby one variable is the dependent variable and the other is the independent variable.

2. How is simple regression used for testing hypotheses? What test statistic is used, and how is it defined?

Simple regression involves estimating the relationship between variables through a straight line (regression line), $Y = a + bX$, where a is the intercept (or constant), and b is the slope. The slope is also called the regression coefficient. If the slope is statistically different from zero, then a relationship is said to exist between the variables in the population. To determine whether the slope equals zero, a t-test is performed. The test statistic is defined as the slope (b) divided by the standard error of the slope ($se[b]$).

3. What is the interpretation of the coefficient of determination, R-square (R^2), and what values can it assume?

R-square can assume values between 0 and +1. The value of R-square is interpreted as the percentage of variation in the dependent variable that is explained by the independent variable.

4. Why is linearity important in regression analysis?

Regression analysis estimates the relationship between variables as a straight line over the *entire range* of observations. If the pattern is curved (for example, parabolic) or broken (for example, upward sloping for one part of the observations and downward sloping for the rest), the assumption of linearity is violated, and the statistical significance of regression coefficients will be underestimated.

5. What is the difference between the observed and predicted values of the dependent variable? What is the error term?

The predicted value of Y (defined, based on the regression model, as $Y = a + bX$) is typically different from the actual observed value of Y. The predicted value of the dependent variable Y is sometimes indicated as $\hat{Y}$ (pronounced "Y-hat"). The difference between Y and $\hat{Y}$ is called the regression error or error term (e). Hence, $Y = \hat{Y} + e$.

6. What is Pearson's correlation coefficient, r? What values can it assume, and how is it interpreted?

Pearson's correlation coefficient, r, measures the association between two continuous variables. It does not distinguish between a dependent and an independent variable, as does simple regression. Pearson's correlation coefficient ranges from -1 to $+1$. The sign indicates the direction of the relationship, which is the same sign as the slope coefficient. Values of r^2 between 0.0 and 0.20 indicate weak associations, values between 0.20 and 0.40 indicate moderate associations, values between 0.40 and 0.65 indicate strong associations, and values above 0.65 are considered to indicate very strong associations. For the two-variable, simple regression model, $r^2 = R^2$.

7. *How is the Pearson's correlation coefficient, r, different from the slope (regression coefficient), b?*

Comparison of the measures r and b (the slope) sometimes causes confusion. Pearson's correlation coefficient, r, indicates not the regression slope but rather the extent to which observations lie close to it. A steep regression line (large b) can have observations that lie either loosely or closely scattered around it, as can a shallow (more horizontal) regression line.

8. *What purpose does Spearman's rank order correlation coefficient (ρ) serve?*

Spearman's rank order correlation coefficient, ρ, is a nonparametric alternative to simple regression and Pearson's correlation coefficient, r. Spearman's rank order correlation coefficient looks at correlation among the ranks of the data rather than among the values. Because Spearman's rank correlation coefficient examines correlation among the ranks of variables, it can also be used with ordinal-level data. Spearman's rank correlation coefficient has a "percent variation explained" interpretation, similar to the other measures described here.

CRITICAL THINKING

1. Explain why variables are assumed to be linearly related in simple regression.

_____

_____

_____

_____

_____

2. Explain why the slope can be used as a test of the relationship of two variables in simple regression.

_____

_____

_____

_____

_____

3. Explain why, if b is statistically significant, then r should be statistically significant, too.

_____

_____

_____

_____

4. Draw a scatterplot between two variables that has a large r^2 and a small, negative b. Then, draw another scatterplot that has a small r^2 and a large, positive b. Show the regression lines in each.

5. You are a program manager for a welfare agency and want to know if a relationship exists between the length of time that people receive welfare (in months) and their education (total years). Both variables are continuous. Table W12.1 is the hypothetical output from your simple regression model. Interpret the results.

_____
_____
_____
_____
_____

Table W12.1 ———〰— Simple Regression Output

R	R-square	SEE
0.002	0.000	1.125

Dependent variable: Unemployment duration

Coefficients

Model	Unstandardized coefficients		t	Sig.
	b	SE		
Constant	0.6710	0.034	19.63	0.000
Education	0.0015	0.033	0.045	0.965

Note: SE = standard error; Sig. = significance.

6. Explain how Spearman's rank coefficient transforms interval-level values into ranks. Then explain why the Spearman's rank coefficient can also be used with ordinal-level variables.

_____
_____
_____
_____
_____

DATA-BASED EXERCISES

1. Use the Productivity dataset. Examine the bivariate relationship between having authority (Jobauthr) and knowledge (Jobknowl) to do one's job. What are your findings? Use simple regression.

_____
_____
_____
_____
_____

2. Use the Productivity dataset. Examine the bivariate relationship between employees' perception of productivity and the perceptions of having adequate authority to do one's job (Jobauthr). Use both simple regression and Pearson's correlation coefficient.

_____
_____
_____
_____
_____

3. Examine the normality of variables used in the preceding exercises (see Chapter 11). Are Jobauthr, Productivity, and Jobknowl normally distributed? On what basis do you reach this conclusion. Is there any transformation that can make them normal?

_____
_____
_____
_____
_____

4. Use the Community Indicators dataset. Which variables are associated with median household incomes?

_____
_____
_____
_____
_____

5. Use the Community Indicators dataset. Create the variables "Cancers per capita" and "Rapes per capita." Which variables are associated with these variables?

_____
_____
_____
_____
_____

6. Visit the CQ Press Web site (psrm.cqpress.com/data_resources.html) for some downloadable data. Open the State Political and Economic Variables dataset. Which variables are associated with voter turnout and political competition?

_____
_____
_____
_____
_____

7. Use the Productivity dataset. Compare employees' perceptions of productivity with those of the outside consultant (Wkctrpro). What test statistic might you use for this comparison?

_____
_____
_____
_____
_____

FURTHER READING

Many books mentioned in the previous chapters also discuss simple regression and the other statistics described here. By now, you may have found one or two other statistics texts that you find useful, and these are likely to discuss these statistics as well. In the next chapter, we identify some further readings for multiple regression, and these books typically also discuss simple regression.

CHAPTER

13

Q & A

1. For what purpose is multiple regression used?

Multiple regression is used to examine the effect of control variables on the relationship between one dependent variable and one (or more) independent variables.

2. What is full model specification? How does full model specification relate to a nomothetic mode of explanation?

Full model specification means that analysts attempt to identify *all of the variables* that affect a dependent variable. Fully specified models have two parts: (1) the identification of *the most important factors* that affect a dependent variable (these are independent variables) and (2) the identification of *all other factors* that affect the dependent variable, whose cumulative effects are contained in the error term. The identification of the most important factors is called a nomothetic mode of explanation.

3. What key assumption is made about the error term in regression? How is this assumption examined?

The error term is interpreted as the effect on Y of all other influences on Y that are *not included* as independent variables in the regression model. A key assumption is that the cumulative effect of these independent variables on the regression is zero. Examination of this assumption is based on plots of the standardized residuals against the standardized predicted variable. When the cumulative effect of the error term is zero, its pattern is randomly distributed around (0,0) of the error term plot.

4. How many independent variables are commonly identified in multiple regression? What is the relationship among independent variables?

Multiple regression models typically have five to seven independent variables, although some have many more. Independent variables should be the most important factors that affect the dependent variable. Correlations among independent variables should be low.

5. What is the interpretation of regression coefficients in multiple regression?

In multiple regression, the regression coefficients are interpreted as their effect on the dependent variable, controlled for the effect of all other independent variables included in the regression.

6. What undesirable property does the coefficient of determination, R-square (R^2), have in multiple regression, and how is this problem overcome?

R-square is interpreted as the percentage of variation in the dependent variable that is explained by the independent variable(s). R-square has the undesirable property that it increases with the number of independent variables included in the regression model. Adjusted R-square ($\overline{R}^2$) controls for the number of independent variables in the regression, and is always equal to or less than R-square.

7. *What are standardized coefficients (beta values)? Why are they used?*

Beta values (or betas) are standardized regression coefficients. Beta (β) is defined as the change produced in the dependent variable by a unit of change in the independent variable when both are measured in terms of standard deviation units. Betas are unitless, allowing analysts to compare the impact of different independent variables on the dependent variable. It is appropriate to compare betas across independent variables in the same regression model but not across different models.

8. *What is the function of the global F-test in multiple regression?*

The global F-test examines the overall effect of all independent variables jointly on the dependent variable. The null hypothesis is that the overall effect of all independent variables jointly on the dependent variables is statistically insignificant. The alternate hypothesis is that this overall effect is statistically signficiant. The null hypothesis implies that none of the regression coefficients is statistically significant, that is, $b_1 = b_2 = \ldots = 0$; the alternate hypothesis implies that at least one of the regression coefficients is statistically significant.

9. *What are dummy variables? Why are they useful? Give an example of the use of dummy variables.*

Dummy variables allow researchers to use nominal-level variables in multiple regression. Dummy variables are variables that only have values of one or zero. See Table 13.2 in the textbook for an example of recoding. The number of dummy variables equals the number of measurement categories *minus one.*

10. *Why are regression assumptions so important?*

When the assumptions of multiple regression are violated, the results of multiple regression may be invalid.

11. *Name six assumptions of multiple regression.*

1. No observation is an outlier.
2. No multicollinearity is present among the independent variables.
3. The relationships between the independent variables and the dependent variable are linear.
4. The error term is homoscedastic across the range of each independent variable.
5. Error terms are not serially correlated (or autocorrelated).
6. Variables are measured and specified accurately.

12. *Explain the concept of outliers and how they may affect the results of multiple regression. Also, explain how outliers are detected and how the problem of outliers is remedied.*

Outliers are observations with unusual values that may affect the statistical significance of regression coefficients, notably by influencing the regression slope. Outliers are detected by the size of their error term. Specifically, they are observations whose error terms either exceed +3 standard deviations or are less than –3 standard deviations. The problem of outliers usually is remedied by excluding such observations from analysis.

13. *Explain the concept of multicollinearity and how it affects the results of multiple regression. Also, explain how multicollinearity is detected and how the problem of multicollinearity is remedied.*

Multicollinearity is the problem of two or more independent variables that are so highly correlated that their individual effects on the dependent variable are statistically indistinguishable. Multicollinearity affects the results of multiple regression by causing the regression coefficients of multicollinear variables to be insignificant. Multicollinearity is usually first suspected when regression coefficients are insignificant, even though in bivariate analysis they are known to be highly significant. Multicollinearity is detected formally by variance inflation factor (VIF) scores that exceed 5 or 10. Multicollinearity is remedied by combining substantively related variables into a single index variable, by dropping a collinear variable, or by replacing one variable by a substantively similar but empirically dissimilar variable.

14. Explain the importance of linearity. How is curvilinearity detected, and how is it remedied?

Multiple regression assumes that independent variables are *linearly* correlated with the dependent variable. When relationships are nonlinear (such as being curvilinear), regression coefficients underestimate the significance of the relationship. In some instances, the regression coefficient will be estimated as being insignificant when it is not. Diagnosis of curvilinear relationships centers on examining a curvilinear pattern of the error terms. Curvilinearity is typically corrected by transforming the independent variable with which the dependent variable is curvilinearly related.

15. What is heteroscedasticity? How does it affect the results of multiple regression? How can we detect and remedy heteroscedasticity?

Heteroscedasticity is the problem of unequal variances of the error term. Unequal variances of the error term violate the assumption of the random distribution of the error term and cause the statistical significance of regression coefficients to be underestimated. Heteroscedasticity is graphically detected by examining the error term plot for unequal variances. Error terms are also plotted against each independent variable to determine which dependent-independent variable relationship is heteroscedastic. Often, a logarithmic transformation of both the dependent and independent variables sufficiently corrects the problem.

16. Explain the concept of autocorrelation. How can it affect the results of multiple regression? Also, explain how autocorrelation is detected and how it is remedied.

Adjacent, time-ordered values of observations are usually highly correlated with each other: knowledge of today's value is a good predictor of tomorrow's. Autocorrelation (also called serial correlation) increases the significance of regression coefficients. Autocorrelation can be detected by plotting the error term against time. It is formally detected by testing the Durbin-Watson test statistic: values close to 2 indicate the absence of serial correlation, whereas values closer to 0 and 4 may indicate serial correlation. Two approaches to correcting for serial correlation are (1) to add a trend variable to the model and (2) to test the model in first-order difference form.

17. Why is accurate measurement important in multiple regression?

Multiple regression assumes that variables are measured accurately; variables should be substantively valid and free from any systematic biases. Accurate measurement is especially important for the dependent variable because inaccurate measurement may render it impossible for independent variables to achieve requisite levels of statistical significance.

18. Explain the importance of neither omitting relevant variables nor including irrelevant variables.

The effect of *omitting a relevant variable* is to inflate the value of t-test test statistics of independent variables that are included. The omitted variable is a relevant control variable. The effect of *including irrelevant variables* is the opposite, to understate the importance of other independent variables. Theoretically irrelevant variables cannot be justified, no matter how statistically significant they may be.

CRITICAL THINKING

1. Evaluate and explain the following statement: "Multiple regression is no substitute for bivariate analysis."

    _____

    _____

    _____

    _____

    _____

2. You are a program manager for a welfare agency. In workbook Chapter 12, Critical Thinking Exercise 5, you examined the relationship between the length of time that people receive welfare (in months) and their education (total years). Now you want to consider other variables that might also affect the length of unemployment. Table W13.1 lists categories of different factors that are hypothesized to be the most important in affecting the length of unemployment. Interpret and write up your results.

_____

_____

_____

_____

_____

Table W13.1 ⎯⎯⎯⎯⎯〰⎯ Multiple Regression Output

Model

R	R-square	Adjusted R^2	SEE
0.660	0.435	0.423	0.092

Dependent variable: Unemployment duration

ANOVA Table

Model	Sum of squares	df	Mean square	F	Sig.
Regression	6.294	5	1.259	146.867	0.000
Residual	2.726	318	0.008		
Total	9.020	323			

Coefficients

Model	Unstandardized coefficients		Standardized coefficients	t	Sig.
	b	SE	Beta		
Constant	0.231	.030		7.740	0.000
Receives job training	−0.010	.004	−0.088	−2.579	0.010
Marital status[a]	−0.072	.017	−0.830	−4.125	0.000
Medical condition	0.013	.005	0.140	2.540	0.012
Number of dependents	0.000	.001	0.008	0.252	0.802
Education	−0.003	.003	−0.030	−0.834	0.405

Note: SEE = standard error of the estimate; SE = standard error; Sig. = significance.
[a] Marital Status: 1 = married; 0 = not married.

3. Develop a fully specified model of the factors that affect fund-raising at a nonprofit, social services organization. Focus on different categories of factors that affect fund-raising, and consider how some might be grouped as index variables.

_____

_____

_____

_____

_____

4. Develop a fully specified model of the factors that affect teenage violence in high schools.

_____

_____

_____

_____

_____

_____

5. Explain how regression can be used for prediction. What problem do you see with predicting dependent variable values based on independent variable values that lie outside the range of observations that have been used to estimate the model?

_____

_____

_____

_____

_____

_____

6. Consider a hypothetical variable *Race*, that is coded as 1 = Caucasian, 2 = Native American, 3 = African-American, 4 = Asian or Pacific Islander, and 5 = Other. Recode this variable as a dummy variable that indicates whether the respondent is Caucasian.

_____

_____

_____

_____

_____

_____

7. Explain in your own words why the error term plot should show a random pattern. Also, which variables are shown on the axes?

_____

_____

_____

_____

_____

_____

8. Discuss, in practical terms, how analysts determine which observations are outliers. Discuss also how you would justify the deletion of observations that are outliers.

_____

_____

_____

_____

_____

_____

9. **Draw an error term plot that shows the presence of an outlier (without peeking in the textbook!).**

10. **If two variables are highly correlated with each other (for example, $r^2 = 0.65$), does it follow that they are multicollinear, as well?**

   _____

   _____

   _____

   _____

   _____

   _____

11. **Explain the problem of including irrelevant variables.**

   _____

   _____

   _____

   _____

   _____

   _____

12. **Explain why time series often leads to correlated error terms.**

   _____

   _____

   _____

   _____

   _____

   _____

DATA-BASED EXERCISES

1. Consider the model shown in Table 13.1 of the textbook. In the Productivity dataset, the dependent is Productivity, and the independent variables are labeled, respectively, Teamwork, Jobknowl, Jobauthr, Wrkdyssk, and Recogawd. After you rerun the model shown in Table 13.1, create dummy variables for each of the four departments, and add to the model dummy variables for the first three departments. Are departments associated with employees' perceptions of productivity controlled for all other factors of the model? If yes, which departments are significantly associated with employees' perceptions of productivity? Record your answers on a separate sheet.

2. Use the Public Perceptions dataset. Examine a multiple regression model in which the dependent variable is Posview ("I have a positive view of Orange County"). The independent variables are Quality ("The quality of life in Orange County is good"), Interest ("I believe that the county is interested in what I have to say"), Respect ("The employees treated me with courtesy and respect"), Trust ("Do you trust Orange County to do what is right most of the time?"), and Works ("Do you believe that Orange County works efficiently?"). Examine the error term plot, and write up your findings. Record your answers on a separate sheet.

3. Regarding the model in Exercise 2, consider the effects of race and Hispanic origin on having a positive view. Do race and Hispanic origin affect overall perceptions, when controlled for other variables mentioned in the earlier exercise? Record your answers on a separate sheet.

4. Use the Time dataset. This exercise illustrates the problem of outliers. In this exercise, we examine the effect of water pollution on the concentration of fish in a lake. The dataset contains two variables, Fishcon (the concentration of fish) and Contam1 (the concentration of a water pollutant). The observations are drawn from different parts of a large lake in order to test the hypothesis that alleged water pollution is affecting the stock of fish.

   a. Examine and discuss whether the variables Fishcon and Contam1 are approximately normally distributed.

   _____

   _____

   _____

   _____

   _____

   b. Make a scatterplot of Fishcon and Contam1 for the purpose of getting a visual read of the relationship. Is the relationship positive or negative? Is it strong or weak? Are there any possible outliers? Print the output, and write up your answers.

   _____

   _____

   _____

   _____

   _____

   c. Based on your visual read, you wish to test the hypothesis that the two variables are related. Conduct a simple regression, with Fishcon as the dependent variable. Examine the error term plot for possible outliers. What do you conclude?

   _____

   _____

   _____

   _____

d. Identify the outlier, and eliminate it from subsequent analysis. Provide a write-up of the modified analysis that includes: (1) the hypothesis, (2) the relationship between the variables ($y = ax + b$), (3) the identification and removal of outliers, (4) the correlation and percentage of variance explained (r and r^2), and (5) a plot of the standardized residuals against the predicted values of the dependent variable.

_____

_____

_____

_____

_____

_____

5. **Use the Time dataset. This exercise illustrates the use of dummy variables and includes a test of multicollinearity. The dataset contains observations from 35 hypothetical cities regarding the use of citizen focus groups in various departments (Focus). The data are based on a survey. Most variables are index variables taken from different survey questions. The variables are defined as follows:**

Focus = A composite measure of the breadth and depth of the use of citizen focus groups in a city. Varies from 0 (low) to 20 (high).

Mgrint = A measure of the interest of the city manager in obtaining citizen-based feedback. Varies from 1 (low) to 4 (high).

Pubcompl = A measure of public complaints about the quality and effectiveness of a wide range of municipal services. Varies from 1 (low) to 8 (high).

Budget = Indicates whether municipal budgets have increased in the past two years. Values are –1 = decrease in budget; 0 = no change in budget; 1 = increase in budget.

Size = City size. Varies from 1 = small to 7 = large.

Region = An indicator variable of the region in which the city is located. Values: 1 = Northeast; 2 = South; 3 = Midwest; 4 = West.

In this analysis, you wish to understand which variables cause cities to use citizen-based focus groups.

a. Briefly state your hypotheses.

_____

_____

_____

_____

_____

_____

b. Provide a brief description of variables (univariate analysis). Also, examine the bivariate associations between Focus and Mgrint, Pubcompl, Budget, and Size. Examine the bivariate relationships that exist between all possible pairs of these variables.

_____

_____

_____

_____

_____

_____

c. Examine whether Mgrint, Pubcompl, Budget, and Size are statistically associated with the use of focus groups. For this purpose, conduct a multiple regression in which the dependent variable is Focus and the independent variables are Mgrint, Pubcompl, Budget, and Size. What do you conclude? (You need not write up these results.)

_____

_____

_____

_____

_____

d. You now wish to include the effect of region in your analysis. To do this, you must make Region a dummy variable. Assume you wish to compare the effect of the different regions with Midwest. To make the dummy variables for the Northeast, South, and West, you must either recode the data for each region or enter the data manually. Through either of these techniques, add Northeast, South, and West to your model and rerun the analysis.

_____

_____

_____

_____

_____

e. Provide a complete write-up of the regression. Identify which variables are significant and at what level. Identify the adjusted R-square statistic (is it a strong or weak association?). Also, discuss the beta coefficients. What do you conclude? (2) Plot the standardized residuals against the standardized predicted values. What do you conclude? (3) To examine the possibility of multicollinearity, examine the bivariate correlations among the independent variables. What do you conclude? Given the significance of coefficients, is multicollinearity a problem here?

_____

_____

_____

_____

_____

6. **Use the Time dataset. This exercise illustrates the problem of nonlinearity. It is commonly hypothesized that crimes are more frequent in large cities. The dataset contains the following variables:**

Nvcrime = Index of nonviolent crimes in a given year.

Citysize = City size.

a. To test the above hypothesis, regress Nvcrime as a function of Citysize. Plot the standardized error term against the standardized predicted values and observe the curvilinear (parabolic) slope of the error terms.

_____

_____

_____

_____

_____

b. You suspect that this problem occurs because the relationship between the variables is nonlinear. To examine this possibility, plot Nvcrime against Citysize. Notice the faint rounded curve. Based on the nature of the curve, you decide that a transformation of Citysize is required. You decide to try a square root of Citysize. Make a square root transformation of Citysize. To evaluate the success of this transformation, plot the transformed variable, called TCity (on the X-axis) against Nvcrime (on the Y-axis). Is the relationship still nonlinear? Was the transformation successful?

_____

_____

_____

_____

_____

c. Next, rerun the regression using the transformed variable TCity. Hence, Nvcrime = f(TCity). Reevaluate the residuals by plotting the error term of the transformed model against the transformed independent variable, TCity. What pattern, if any, do you see? If the transformation was unsuccessful, try a log transformation. Do you see a pattern now?

_____

_____

_____

_____

_____

FURTHER READING

Many statistics books discuss regression analysis, including those mentioned in previous chapters of this workbook. However, some of these discussions are a little superficial. For a brief introduction, see Larry Gonick and Woollcott Smith, *The Cartoon Guide to Statistics* (New York: HarperPerennial, 1994), or Sam Kash Kachigan, *Multivariate Statistical Analysis: A Conceptual Introduction,* 2d ed. (New York: Radius Press, 1991).

For a more solid introduction, try William M. Mendenhall, *A Second Course in Statistics: Regression Analysis,* 6th ed. (Upper Saddle River, N.J.: Prentice Hall, 2003). Another good presentation is found in David G. Kleinbaum et al., *Applied Regression Analysis and Multivariable Methods* (Pacific Grove, Calif.: Duxbury Press, 1998). Try also J. McKee and J. McClendon, *Multiple Regression and Causal Analysis* (Long Grove, Ill.: Waveland Press, 2002).

The following books are a little advanced but also quite useful. Two classic textbooks with an economics orientation are Robert Pindyck and Daniel Rubinfield, *Econometric Models and Economic Forecasts,* 3d ed. (New York: McGraw-Hill, 1997), and Damodar Gujarati, *Basic Econometrics,* 4th ed. (New York: McGraw-Hill, 2002). A well-respected general social science book is John Neter et al., *Applied Linear Statistical Models,* 4th ed. (New York: McGraw-Hill, 1996).

CHAPTER 14

Q & A

1. *When should logistic regression be used? Provide some examples.*

Logistic regression should be used when the dependent variable is dichotomous, that is, when it has only two values. Some typical examples of a dichotomous dependent variable are whether or not someone got elected, whether or not a war occurred, and whether or not a medical event occurred. In these instances, something either happened, or it didn't—a dichotomous situation.

2. *What regression problem does logistic regression address?*

Multiple regression assumes a continuous dependent variable. Logistic regression uses a dichotomous dependent variable, that is, one that has only two values, such as zero and one.

3. *How does the estimation model of logistic regression differ from multiple regression?*

Whereas the multiple regression estimation model uses a straight line, logistic regression uses a logistic curve, which is S-shaped. Both approaches select a model that best fits the observed observations.

4. *What is the log likelihood value, −2LL?*

The log likelihood value, −2LL, is a quantitative measure of how well the model predicts observed values. Better-fitting models have smaller values of | −2LL |.

5. *How is a classification table used to assess the goodness of fit in logistic regression?*

A classification table shows the percentage of corrected predicted observations. The minimum is 50 percent, indicating the lack of any useful prediction. Typically, standards of 80–85 percent indicate good model prediction.

6. *What are Nagelkerke R^2 and Cox and Snell R^2?*

These are measures of association. Higher values imply a better fit. Nagelkerke R^2 has a variance-explained interpretation.

7. *What test is used for the statistical significance of logistic regression coefficients?*

In logistic regression, Wald chi-square is used as a test statistic to determine the statistical significance of logistic regression coefficients.

8. *How can logistic regression coefficients be used to calculate event probabilities?*

The predicted values of logistic regression coefficients can be used to show the probability of an event's occurring, by using the following formula:

$\text{Prob(event)} = 1/[1 + e^{-Z}]$, where $Z = a + b_1X_1 + b_2X_2 + \ldots$.

Z is also called the logit.

9. *What is an odds ratio?*

   An odds ratio is used to compare the probability of something occurring, as compared to it not occurring. One way of using this measure is to observe how the odds ratio changes when only one independent variable is changed, such as by one unit.

CRITICAL THINKING

1. **Identify dichotomous variables that are relevant to your area of interest, and develop a model to predict them.**

   _____
   _____
   _____
   _____
   _____

2. **Explain the following statement: "The dichotomous nature of the dependent variable violates an assumption of multiple regression."**

   _____
   _____
   _____
   _____
   _____

3. **The S-shaped logistic curve has values that lie between 0 and 1. What problem does this address?**

   _____
   _____
   _____
   _____
   _____

4. **Explain why a good model fit will show a Hosmer and Lemeshow test statistic that is insignificant.**

   _____
   _____
   _____
   _____
   _____

5. **Verify the event probability calculations shown in Table 14.2 of the textbook.**

   _____
   _____
   _____
   _____
   _____

6. Table W14.1 shows the output of a logistic model that predicts promotion within five years. Is the model adequate: why, or why not? What is the probability that a 37-year-old female who has a performance appraisal rating of 4 will be promoted? The performance variable (Appraisal) is measured on a scale of 5 = high to 1 = low; Gender is defined as 1 = male, 2 = female; and Age = employee's age (in years).

_____

_____

_____

_____

_____

Table W14.1 ———— Logistic Regression Output

Model Fit

Model	2 log likelihood (–2LL) Sig. (base model)	Cox and Snell R²	Nagelkerke R²	Hosmer and Lemeshow test Chi-square	Sig.
48.253	0.000	0.317	0.428	4.940	0.764

Dependent variable: Promotion

Coefficients

Model	Unstandardized coefficients b	SE	Wald chi-square	Sign.
Constant	–4.016	3.285	1.495	0.221
Gender	–0.532	0.734	0.526	0.468
Appraisal	1.990	0.603	10.878	0.001
Age	–0.082	0.083	0.977	0.323

Classification Table

Observed Variable	Group	Predicted Promotion 0	1	Percentage correct
Promotion	0	23	7	76.7
	1	6	14	70.0
Overall percentage				74.0

Note: Sig. = significance; SE = standard error

7. **Identify one or more research articles that use logistic regression. Record your findings on a separate sheet**

DATA-BASED EXERCISES

1. **Use the Public Perceptions dataset. Predict Trust ("Trust in government") as a function of Interest ("County officials are interested in what I have to say"), Works ("Do you believe the county government works efficiently?"), Quality ("The quality of life in Orange County is good"), and race. To this end, (1) create a dummy variable for race (1 = white, 0 = all others) from the variable Ethnic, and (2) recode the values of "DK" for the variables Trust and Works as missing. Use logistic regression, and report the results.**

Trust = f(Interest, Works, Quality, White)

a. Verify that the dependent variable is dichotomous.

_____

_____

_____

b. Does the model satisfy the standard for correctly predicted observations?

_____

_____

_____

c. Which variables are significant?

_____

_____

_____

d. Calculate event probabilities.

_____

_____

_____

2. **Use the Public Perceptions dataset. Predict Manage ("Doing a good job managing growth") as a function of Works ("Do you believe the county government works efficiently?"), Quality ("The quality of life in Orange County is good"), and Watch ("Watching Orange County TV"). Use logistic regression, and report the results.**

Manage = f(Works, Quality, Watch).

a. Verify that the dependent variable is dichotomous.

_____

_____

_____

b. Does the model satisfy the standard for correctly predicted observations? If not, does it satisfy the Hosmer and Lemeshow test?

_____

_____

_____

c. Which variables are significant?

_____

_____

_____

d. Calculate event probabilities.

_____

_____

_____

3. Political scientists often use logistic regression for modeling factors affecting election outcomes. Some of these datasets are available on-line. Search for these on Google, by using the search string "political elections SPSS data," for example, if you are using SPSS.

   One of the sites that host election datasets is at the University of Essex (England), Project on Political Transformation and the Electoral Process in Post-Communist Europe (www.essex.ac.uk/elections). For example, consider the SPSS dataset regarding Russian candidates in 1999 elections. At this Web site, select Candidate data (from the left scroll bar) → Russia → 1999 SPSS format. (If you do not use SPSS, you should save this file to your computer, and then use your own statistical software program to open the file.) Open the saved file, and predict, for example, factors associated with candidates winning elections. You may need to first transform this variable to 0 = not winning an election and 1 = winning an election, as this dataset distinguishes between being elected in a single-member constituency (coded 1), and being elected from a party list (coded 2). How is being an incumbent associated with winning elections in Russia?

   _____

   _____

   _____

   _____

   _____

4. Visit the University of Michigan Library, "Statistical Resources on the Web Political Science" site (www.lib.umich.edu/govdocs/stpolisc.html#nes). Examine some of the available datasets (for example, on elections). Another resource is the University of California, which makes datasets available through SDA, Survey Documentation & Analysis (http://sda.berkeley.edu:7502/). Explore available datasets through the link "SDA archive." Select any dataset (for example, National Election Survey 1948–2000), and note the option to run logit regression. However, you should first examine the variable descriptions by selecting "Open Extra Codebook Window." You will likely need to recode some of the variables first. You can also download a customized subset of data.

FURTHER READING

Numerous advanced texts are available on the topics discussed in this chapter. For a discussion of logistic regression, see Joseph Hair et al., *Multivariate Data Analysis* (Upper Saddle River, N.J.: Prentice Hall, 1998). This is an advanced, but nonmathematical introduction. Another text is David Hosmer and Stanley Lemeshow, *Applied Logistic Regression* (New York: Wiley, 2000). Many of the previously mentioned texts that discuss regression also cover logistic regression.

The research literature includes many examples of logistic regression. Here are some: John Ishiyama, "Does Globalization Breed Ethnic Conflict?" *Nationalism & Ethnic Politics* 9 (winter 2003): 1–23; Matthew J. Dickinson and Kathryn Dunn Tenpas, "Explaining Increasing Turnover Rates Among Presidential Advisers, 1929–1997" *Journal of Politics* (May 1997): 434–449; P. Edward French, Sangho Moon, and Rodney E. Stanley, "Utilizing Logistic Regression for Explaining Lottery Adoption in the Volunteer State" *International Journal of Public Administration* 27 (2004): 353–367; Marc A. Wallace, "An Analysis of Presidential Preferences in the Distribution of Empowerment Zones and Enterprise Communities," *Public Administration Review* 63 (2003): 562–572. You can readily use databases available through your library to find others.

Q & A

1. What are time series data?

Time series data are data that have been collected over time, such as periodic assessments of performance outcomes or public (or client) opinions.

2. Which regression assumption is usually violated when using time series data? What problem does this cause?

With time series data, the assumption of random distribution of error terms usually is violated. Specifically, the error term plot, when plotted against the sequence of time-ordered observations, typically exhibits a pattern. This is called autocorrelation or serial correlation. The problem with autocorrelation is that it severely exaggerates the statistical significance of variables, leading to the erroneous conclusion that variables are statistically associated when they are not.

3. How is autocorrelation detected?

Autocorrelation can be detected by plotting the error term against time. It is formally detected by testing the Durbin-Watson test statistic: values close to 2 indicate the absence of serial correlation, whereas values closer to 0 and 4 may indicate serial correlation.

4. How is autocorrelation addressed?

Two strategies are available for correcting serial correlation: the first strategy is to add a trend variable to the model, and the second strategy is to examine the relationship in so-called first-order differences. Relationships in first-difference form often eliminate problems of serial correlation because differenced data exhibit far more variability than do levels data. By contrast, adding a trend variable is a prophylactic strategy that attempts to control for the problem. Regression of first-order differences is considered a more stringent test.

5. How is time series regression used for evaluating the impact of policies?

Time series data are excellent for evaluating the impact of a policy or program. Levels of performance or service utilization are tracked and compared with the moment or period in which a policy is implemented.

6. What are policy variables?

Policy variables measure when and how policies affect the dependent variables. Four types of policy variables are those that model pulse, period, step, and increasing impacts.

7. What are lagged variables?

Lagged variables are independent variables that have a lagged effect on the dependent variable.

8. Explain the difference between predicted values and forecasted values.

Predicted values are calculated values (based on the regression coefficients) of the dependent variable that can be compared with the actual (observed) values of the dependent variable. Forecasted values are calculated values of a variable for a future time for which no observed value has yet occurred. Hence, forecasted values cannot be compared with observed values.

9. What strategy is used to validate forecasts?

Forecasts of the current period(s) are made using observations from preceding periods. These forecasts are then compared with actual observations.

10. Name four types of regression-based forecasting.

Regression-based forecasting includes leading indicators, curve estimation, exponential smoothing, and ARIMA.

11. What is forecasting with leading indicators?

Forecasting with leading indicators involves regression with independent variables that are all lagged (leading indicators). These leading indicators are then regarded as harbingers of future change.

12. What is the difference between curve estimation and exponential smoothing?

Curve estimation makes forecasts based only on the level and trend variable. Exponential smoothing uses an iterative estimation process that chooses parameters of level, trend, and seasonality to best fit a model to the observed data.

13. How are periodic effects included in forecasts?

Periodicity is included in forecasts by adjusting mean forecasts to reflect the mean periodicity effects of prior periods.

14. Compare forecasting based on prior moving averages, prior moving changes, and known ratios.

Forecasting based on prior moving averages predicts future values based on the mean of preceding values. Forecasting based on prior moving changes predicts future values based on the immediately preceding value and the mean of preceding increases. Forecasting based on known ratios uses the value of one variable to predict another variable, assuming that both the ratio of variables and an accurate forecast of the other variable are known. Forecasts based on prior moving averages tend to be conservative.

CRITICAL THINKING

1. Give some examples of time series data in your area of interest. Discuss ways in which these data might be analyzed.

_____

_____

_____

_____

2. Explain why autocorrelation is almost always present when using regression analysis with time series data.

_____

_____

_____

3. The Durbin-Watson test statistic for autocorrelation of a regression model with 35 observations and four independent variables is 1.98. What do you conclude? And what would you conclude if the Durbin-Watson test statistic were 1.08?

    _____
    _____
    _____
    _____
    _____

4. Explain the following statement: "The regression of first-order differences is considered a far more stringent test than adding a trend variable."

    _____
    _____
    _____
    _____
    _____

5. Explain how policy variables help to evaluate program effectiveness. Does the magnitude of these dummy variables matter?

    _____
    _____
    _____
    _____
    _____

6. Give an example of an independent variable that you suspect might have a lagged impact on a dependent variable.

    _____
    _____
    _____
    _____
    _____

7. Explain the difference between prediction and forecasting.

    _____
    _____
    _____
    _____
    _____

8. Discuss why prior moving averages (PMA) forecasting may be more conservative than forecasting based on prior average changes.

    _____
    _____
    _____
    _____
    _____

9. Discuss the steps for forecasting with periodic effects with few observations.

_____

_____

_____

_____

_____

10. How might you forecast the revenues of a city? Identify three different approaches.

_____

_____

_____

_____

_____

DATA-BASED EXERCISES

1. Use the Time dataset. This exercise illustrates the autocorrelation problem in the use of policy variables. Time series data are common in program evaluation and public policy. These data examine the impact of a law, which, among other things, increases jail time for those convicted of driving under the influence (DUI). The dataset contains the following variables:

Fatal = Traffic fatalities per 100,000 miles driven.

Year = Year of traffic fatalities measured.

Short = A dummy variable identifying when the policy intervention occurred, namely, in 1980 when a law was passed that requires mandatory jail time for DUI. The values are 0 = pre-law adoption (pre-1980); and 1 = post-law adoption (post-1980).

Long = A dummy variable identifying the number of years of post-policy adoption. The values are 0 for pre-law adoption, and 1 for 1980, 2 for 1981, 3 for 1982, and so forth. This variable gives weight to the long-term effect of policy.

Jailtime = Days of jail time served by offenders as a result of the law.

Note: Although increased jail time is the primary effect of the program, data from other aspects of the program (such as midnight checkpoints) are not available to the researcher. The variables Short and Long model these unknown effects.

a. You wish to evaluate whether the new law has been effective. You model the effect on fatalities and explore the possibility of autocorrelation in time series data. Hence, Fatal = *f*(Short, Long, Jailtime). Run the regression analysis, and examine the error term for autocorrelation. Specifically, examine the Durbin-Watson test statistic. What do you conclude?

_____

_____

_____

_____

b. Now, take the trend variable into account: Add Year as an independent variable to your list. Again, note the Durbin-Watson statistic. What do you conclude about adding the trend variable? Provide a complete write-up.

_____

_____

_____

_____

c. For further rigor, you examine the relationship in first-order differences. Make first-order differences, and examine Δ Fatal = f(Short, Long, Δ Jailtime). What do you conclude? Also, try lagging each of the independent variables for up to two periods. What do you conclude?

_____

_____

_____

_____

_____

2. **Use the Crime dataset. The data are monthly observations of juvenile arrests in a city with a curfew for teenagers. The curfew prohibits teenagers from being outside between 8 PM and 1 AM.**

   Note: These data are adapted from actual cities. Although these are monthly data, the same approach can be applied to weekly or daily data. In those cases, rather than controlling periodicity by month, control variables control for periodicity by week or day.

   a. Plot the number of juvenile arrests (Juvarsts) over time. What do you conclude about the impact of the curfew? What factors might underlie the periodicity?

_____

_____

_____

_____

_____

   b. Run the regression of Curfew against Juvarsts. What do you conclude from the Durbin-Watson statistic? To attempt to correct for autocorrelation, include both the year and each of the months as control variables. Run the model in both levels and first-order difference forms, hence:

$$\text{Juvarsts} = f(\text{Curfew, Month 1 – Month 11, Year}), \text{ and}$$
$$\Delta \text{Juvarsts} = f(\Delta\text{Curfew, Month 1 – Month 11, Year}).$$

   Which of these models deals with the problem of autocorrelation? Why is Month 12 excluded from the model?

_____

_____

_____

_____

_____

c. It is sometimes noted in the literature that law enforcement displaces crime rather than reduces it. Rather than committing crimes between 8 PM and 1 AM, juveniles will target other time periods to commit crimes. The dataset includes the variable Crimarst, which measures total monthly juvenile arrests. Run the same models as under item b, with Crimarst as the dependent variable. What do you conclude?

_____

_____

_____

_____

_____

3. Table W15.1 shows expenditures for the past five years. Forecast the next three periods using (1) prior moving averages (three-year spans), and (2) prior average moving changes (with last period as base). Add your forecast to the table.

Table W15.1 ⎯⎯⎯⎯⎯∿∿⎯ Worksheet for Forecasting Based on Prior Moving Changes

Time	Expenditures (current $s)	Inflation (%)	Expenditures (constant $s)	Increase	Avg. changes	Forecasts
1	100	4.1	?	—	—	—
2	102	3.0	?	?	—	—
3	108	2.4	114.1	?	—	—
4	112	3.2	115.6	?	?	—
5	116	—	116.0	?	?	?
6	—	—	—	?	?	?
7	—	—	—	?	?	?
8	—	—	—	—	—	?

4. Table W15.2 shows attendance data of a public museum. Make a worksheet for calculating forecasts based on (1) prior moving averages and (2) prior moving changes for the next five periods. Also, validate your forecasts by comparing actual and predicted values.

_____

_____

_____

_____

_____

Table W15.2 ⎯⎯⎯⎯⎯∿∿⎯ Public Museum Attendance

Time	Attendance	Time	Attendance
1	1,205	9	1,468
2	1,309	10	1,602
3	1,325	11	1,625
4	1,226	12	1,698
5	1,450	13	1,550
6	1,529	14	1,623
7	1,679	15	1,708
8	1,543	16	1,767

5. Use linear regression to forecast museum attendance based on the data provided in the preceding exercise.

_____

_____

_____

_____

_____

6. Daily workload activities are shown in Table W15.3. Forecast workloads for Week 5.

_____

_____

_____

_____

_____

Table W15.3 ———————— Daily Workload Activity

Day	Workload	Day	Workload	Day	Workload
1	63	6	70	11	69
2	72	7	77	12	75
3	76	8	75	13	77
4	67	9	72	14	70
5	53	10	50	15	62

7. Use the Crime dataset. (1) Create a new variable, Juvars2, which is the number of juvenile arrests between 8 PM and 1 AM (Juvarsts) *prior* to the curfew. (2) Use curve estimation to forecast future arrest rates. Using alternative models, what do you conclude about likely future arrest rates? (3) To include periodicity effects, try to forecast using exponential smoothing. (*Note:* This procedure is not available on all statistical software.) Record your findings on a separate sheet.

8. A regulatory analyst examines violations. The data in Table W15.4 show the occurrence of the first violation as a function of the number of years of being in business. Create a spreadsheet that reflects these data and determine the probability of violation in each period.

_____

_____

_____

_____

_____

Table W15.4 ———————— First Violations as a Function of Years in the Business

Year	No. of businesses	No. of violations
0	10	0
1	12	8
2	15	2
3	18	3
4	24	2
5	12	4
6	15	1

FURTHER READING

Discussions of time series regression tend to be heavily mathematical, but many textbooks do provide a good conceptual foundation. See William M. Mendenhall, *A Second Course in Statistics: Regression Analysis,* 6th ed. (Upper Saddle River, N.J.: Prentice Hall, 2003). Some useful chapters are in Gerald Miller and Marcia Whicker, *Handbook of Research Methods in Public Administration* (New York: Marcel Dekker, 1999), chaps. 14 through 16. You can also look for articles using time series regression in your field of interest.

For forecasting, see S. Makradakis, *Forecasting* (New York: John Wiley & Sons, 1998). Also, SPSS, *Trends 10.0* (Chicago: SPSS, Inc., 1999), provides numerous illustrations and examples. The Trends module is marketed separately from other software. Forecasting, as discussed here, is also found in Murray Spiegel and Larry Stephens, *Statistics: Schaum's Outline Series* (New York: McGraw-Hill, 1998). You can also look at examples of forecasting, such as U.S. Congressional Budget Office, *The Budget and Economic Outlook: Fiscal Years 2006 to 2015* (Washington, D.C.: U.S. Congressional Budget Office, 2005).

Q & A

1. For what purpose is ANOVA used?

ANOVA is used for testing whether three or more groups have different means and, if so, which groups have different means. By comparison, t-tests are used for testing whether two groups have different means.

2. What is the purpose of the global F-test in ANOVA?

The ANOVA global F-test tests for differences among any of the means.

3. What is a post-hoc test? Name three post-hoc tests.

Post-hoc tests are tests that test all possible group differences and do so in a manner that maintains a true (5 percent or 1 percent) level of significance. Three popular post-hoc tests are Tukey, Bonferroni, and Scheffe. The Scheffe test is the most conservative, the Tukey test is best when many comparisons are made (that is, there are many groups), and the Bonferroni test is preferred when few comparisons are made.

4. What are the four test assumptions for ANOVA?

(1) One variable is continuous, and the other variable is ordinal or nominal.
(2) The group distributions have equal variances.
(3) Observations are independent.
(4) The variable is normally distributed in each of the groups.

5. How can ANOVA test the linearity of relationships that involve a continuous variable and an ordinal variable?

ANOVA can also be used to test the linearity of interval-ordinal relationships, that is, whether the change in means follows a linear, an increasing, or a decreasing pattern according to the ordering of the ordinal variable. The appropriate F-test is the statistic reported as the "linear term for unweighted sum of squares" in ANOVA tables.

6. What is MANOVA? How is it different from two-way ANOVA?

MANOVA is a technique for analyzing the effects of multiple independent variables on multiple dependent variables. Two-way ANOVA is a technique for analyzing the effects of two independent variables on one dependent variable.

7. What is path analysis, and what advantage does it offer over multiple regression?

Path analysis is a causal modeling technique. Unlike multiple regression, path analysis allows for direct and indirect effects of variables. Path analysis is a recursive causal modeling technique, that is, one that does not allow feedback loops.

8. *How are paths estimated?*

Each path is estimated separately using regression (ordinary least squares, or OLS).

9. *What is an exogenous variable? What is an endogenous variable? What purpose do these terms serve?*

Causal modeling distinguishes between *exogenous* variables, which are variables that are unaffected by other variables in the model, and *endogenous* variables, which are affected by other variables. The distinction is useful because in causal models variables can be both independent and dependent.

10. *What assumptions must path analysis models satisfy?*

Path analysis must satisfy all OLS assumptions (see Chapter 1 in the textbook). In addition, all error terms must be uncorrelated with all exogenous variables. As in regression, the model must be theory based.

11. *How are direct and indirect effects of variables calculated?*

Direct effects are simply the beta coefficients of the variables that immediately affect another variable. Indirect effects are calculated as the product of beta coefficients of each pathway. See Table 16.3 in the textbook for an example of such calculations.

12. *What is a structural equation model, and how is it different from path analysis?*

Structural equation models simultaneously estimate relationships among observed variables and factor constructs. Unlike path analysis, structural equation models may involve feedback loops. Models with feedback loops are called nonrecursive.

13. *What are censored data? Give an example.*

Censored observations are those for which the specified outcomes have yet to occur. For example, in a study of student retention, some students have not (yet) dropped out of the program but may still do so before they graduate.

14. *What is the purpose of a life table?*

Life tables show the probability of a dichotomous event's occurring for each time period.

15. *What is factor analysis?*

Factor analysis is an exploratory technique that groups variables together based on their similarities and dissimilarities. Similarly grouped variables may suggest variables for subsequent index construction.

16. *What four steps does factor analysis involve?*

(1) Determining that the group of variables has enough correlation to allow for factor analysis
(2) Determining how many factors should be used for classifying (or grouping) the variables
(3) Improving the interpretation of correlations and factors (through a process called rotation)
(4) Naming the factors and, possibly, creating index variables for subsequent analysis

CRITICAL THINKING

1. Your data include a measure of air pollution that is measured on a continuous scale, as well as another variable that measures the location of that air pollution in five counties. Which test statistic should you use to examine whether mean pollution levels vary across counties?

_____

_____

_____

_____

_____

2. Table W16.1 is a sample output ANOVA table with linearity test. Interpret the output.

_____
_____
_____
_____
_____

Table W16.1 ⎯⎯⎯∿⎯ ANOVA Table with Linearity Test

			Sum of squares	df	Variance (s^2)	F-test	p
Between groups	Combined		12.041	3	4.014	2.797	.043
	Linear term	Unweighted	7.701	1	7.701	5.367	.022
		Weighted	7.482	1	7.482	5.215	.024
		Deviation	4.558	2	2.279	1.588	.209
Within groups			162.137	113	1.435		
Total			174.178	116			

3. Draw a recursive causal model (path analysis) of factors that increase student success, measured as graduation. Which variables are direct influences, which are indirect influences, and which, if any, are both? Be sure to indicate clearly the direct and indirect influences on the dependent variable.

4. Figure W16.1 shows the results of a path analysis. The values above the paths are beta coefficients. Which variable has the largest influence?

_____

Figure W16.1⎯⎯⎯∿⎯Path Analysis with Beta Coefficients

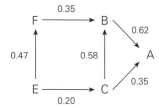

5. Give three examples of situations that may involve censored data.

_____
_____
_____
_____
_____

6. Do censored data necessarily involve data that are collected over time?

7. Give an example of a leading indicator of crime that might be used in regression-based forecasting.

8. Consider the trend shown in Figure W16.2. Should forecasting involve periodicity, and, if so, what period of time should be considered? What is the consequence of not using periodicity?

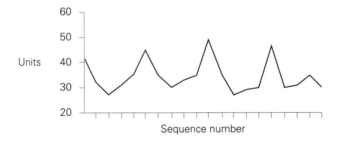

Figure W16.2 ──────── ╱╲╱─ Trend

DATA-BASED EXERCISES

1. Use the Public Perceptions dataset. An analyst wants to know whether the index variable of customer service varies across race. Recode the variable Ethnic to distinguish among whites, blacks, other races, and Hispanics, and then calculate the means for each of these groups. Then use ANOVA to determine whether any of these differences are statistically significant.

2. Use the Public Perceptions dataset. An analyst wants to know whether incomes vary by age groups. Treat the income variable as a continuous variable, and treat the age variable as an ordinal-grouping

variable. Calculate the means for each of these groups, and then use ANOVA to determine whether any of these differences are statistically significant. For which age groups is the relationship linear?

_____

_____

_____

_____

_____

3. Use the Productivity dataset. Create a path analysis of the model shown in Figure W16.3. Does the model meet the condition of not having feedback loops? Begin by specifying (that is, identifying) all of the regression models that are to be estimated. For each, identify the dependent and independent variables. Then estimate ("run") the models, record the beta coefficients, and calculate direct and indirect effects.

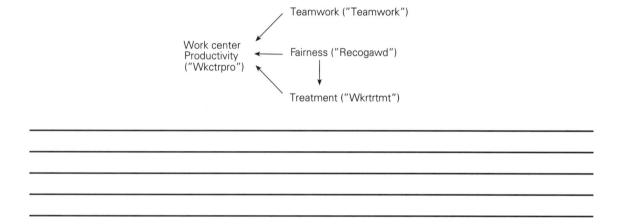

Figure W16.3——————⌇⋀⋁⋏⌇——"Productivity" Path Analysis

_____

_____

_____

_____

_____

FURTHER READING

Numerous books discuss ANOVA. See Sam Kash Kachigan, *Multivariate Statistical Analysis: A Conceptual Introduction,* 2d ed. (New York: Radius Press, 1991); Chapter 5 provides a most lucent discussion of ANOVA. The *SPSS Base Applications Guide* has an excellent, practical discussion, and carries this topic further. Analysts in health care settings will want a more detailed discussion, such as in Barbara Tabchnick and Linda Fidell, *Using Multivariate Statistics* (New York: HarperCollins, 1996), or John Neter et al., *Applied Linear Statistical Models* (New York: McGraw-Hill, 1996).

For a discussion of various exploratory techniques, see Sam Kash Kachigan, *Multivariate Statistical Analysis: A Conceptual Introduction,* 2d ed. (New York: Radius Press, 1991). See also Joseph Hair et al., *Multivariate Data Analysis* (Upper Saddle River, N.J.: Prentice Hall, 1998), for a more advanced discussion. This book also has an excellent, introductory chapter on ANOVA.

For survival analysis, see A. A. Affifi and Virginia Clark, *Computer-Aided Multivariate Techniques* (London: Chapman & Hall, 1996); David Hosmer and Stanley Lemeshow, *Applied Survival Analysis: Regression Modeling of Time to Event Data* (New York: John Wiley & Sons, 1999); or *SPSS Advanced Models 10.0* (Chicago: SPSS, Inc., 1999).

For structural equation models, the *AMOS 6.0 User's Guide* (Chicago: SPSS, Inc., 2005) provides a useful introduction and many clear examples. AMOS is very user friendly. A free student download of this software with sample datasets is available at www.amosdevelopment.com. For an example of research using this technique, see Evan Berman and Jonathan West, "The Impact of Revitalized Management Practices on the Adoption of Information Technology: A National Survey of Local Governments," *Public Performance & Management Review* (March 2001): 233–253.

This chapter guides you through the operating characteristics of the Statistical Package for the Social Sciences (SPSS). This popular software is an invaluable tool for social scientists because of its capacity for handling large datasets and performing a wide range of statistical tests. Across many social science professions, including public administration and public policy analysis, SPSS software offers professionals, practitioners, and students alike the ability to perform myriad statistical procedures and data evaluation processes. Even better, it handles these analyses and operations without requiring users to perform intricate mathematical operations. Luckily, SPSS is also extremely easy to use. For those already familiar with various spreadsheet software programs, SPSS looks and feels quite similar. If you don't have previous experience with spreadsheets, there is no need for apprehension, since SPSS is truly user friendly. Through the initial familiarization exercises, you will quickly gain an appreciation of just how simple it is to use this software as a data analysis tool.

Of course, understanding the statistical concepts that underlie the tasks SPSS will perform is crucial. By analogy, if SPSS is viewed as a vehicle, then you are the driver and need to know the rules of the road. The textbook *Essential Statistics for Public Managers and Policy Analysts* is about the rules and practice of using statistics; studying it will help you develop a sense of what you need to look out for—such as data characteristics, causality patterns in relationships, and the assumptions and limitations of various statistical procedures. This chapter helps users get started with SPSS and shows them how to apply concepts discussed in the textbook. Enough said. Now, let's get started!

SPSS SCREENS

After you open SPSS, the Data Editor screen will appear as shown in Screen W17.1. This screen will display the data, values, and labels for each dataset variable. Presently, no data are displayed because you have not yet created or opened a file in SPSS.

At the top of the screen is the toolbar from which SPSS commands are selected. These commands are the principal way of getting your data in shape for subsequent analysis. Note the Help function, which contains a tutorial to introduce you to the capabilities of SPSS. Investigating this tool is certainly worth the time investment and is highly recommended.

Take time to explore each of the toolbar menus and familiarize yourself with the options and functions of each. Don't worry if the terminology seems unfamiliar at first. As you progress through this guide, you will work your way through it.

At the bottom left of the SPSS Data Editor screen are two tabs, called Data View and Variable View. Select the Variable View tab. The screen displayed contains no information beyond the fields comprising that screen because no file has been opened yet. This screen will be explained and demonstrated when you create your first variable.

To return to the Data View screen, merely select the tab at the bottom of the screen. SPSS also has an Output screen that will become familiar to you after you complete your first analysis.

CREATING A VARIABLE

Chapter 6 of the textbook uses sample data in the discussion of the mean, median, and mode. We will use those data to create your first variable and then see how easy it is for SPSS to perform statistical calculations.

Screen W17.1 ———— ⌇⌇⌇ — Data Editor Screen

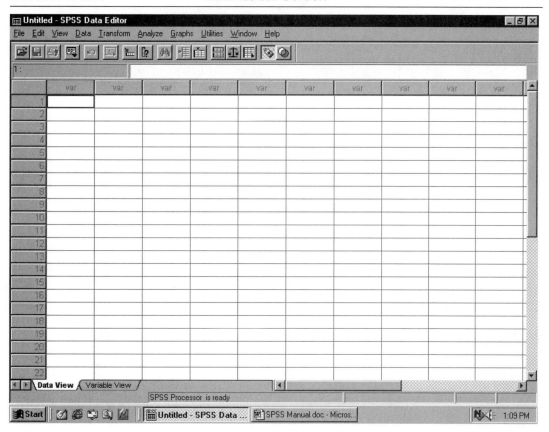

Note: Throughout this guide, the symbol → means "execute the next command immediately following the arrow." For example, Select Variable View → Name means "open the Variable View screen and then select Name by placing the cursor over the Name option and left clicking." Practice this command now.

To create the first variable, we will give it a name and a label. Go to the Variable View screen, and place the cursor in the first row of the cells in the Name column. In the first cell, type "variablx" as shown in Screen W17.2. We could have used a longer name than variablx, but historically variable names in SPSS have been limited to eight characters and many analysts still follow this practice. Variable names must start with a letter and may contain only letters and numbers, as well as periods when not used as the first or last character; thus, "variable x" is not a valid variable name (it contains an empty space), but "variablex" and "var.x" are. Don't worry about remembering what each variable name means; the purpose of the Label column is to fully define the variable name. We will show you how to create labels, too. (Once the label is entered, SPSS will use the label, rather than the variable name, in subsequent output tables.)

Entering the variable name automatically produces some additional settings, as shown in Screen W17.2. The next column allows selection of the type of variable. The default setting for Type is a numeric variable; your variable is numeric, since you will be entering numbers. To examine other options, highlight the cell in the first row of the Type column. This will bring up an icon in the right-hand sector of the data cell. When you click on that icon, you will see a pop-up menu, a typical feature of SPSS, from which you select the type of variable. In the case of variablx, select Numeric. This pop-up dialog box is shown in Screen W17.3. Continuing across, the first cell in the Width column identifies the maximum number of characters of this variable; the default is 8. The Decimals column indicates the number of decimals; the default is 2. Hence, the default settings accommodate any value of variablx up to 99999.99. The Label column provides user-defined fields to further describe each variable. As shown in Screen W17.3, type in the label "Data for calculating mean, median and mode." (Double clicking on the Label data box allows label entry and editing of entries.) In later sections, you will learn more about the Values and Missing columns. The latter column is to the right of the screen, found by using the horizontal scroll bar at the bottom of the screen. The default for

Screen W17.2 ———— ᴡᴡ— Naming Variables

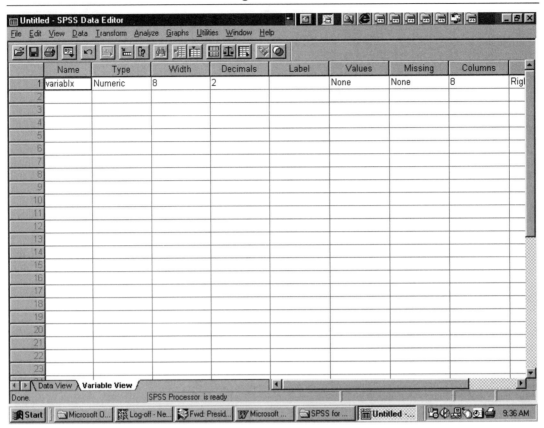

both is "None." The column labeled "Columns" adjusts the widths of the columns in the Data View screen. The widths of the columns in the Variable View screen can also be adjusted by placing the cursor between two columns until you see the icon that is used to adjust the widths of the columns, which looks like this:

On the right-hand side of the Variable View screen, you will see two additional columns. The Align column aligns the data in the Data View screen to the right, left, or center (this is somewhat analogous to the alignment of text in word processing programs). The rightmost column is labeled "Measure." Variables can be labeled as being nominal, ordinal, or scale (that is, continuous). This label is of no consequence in using most SPSS features later, nor does the label appear on most SPSS outputs. Rather, the label shows up on dialog boxes from which variables are selected, such as Screen W17.5. This label may serve as a reminder to analysts of the measurement level of their variables. Here, we define variablx as a scale—the default label, which appears with a ruler icon to the left of the variable name in Screen W17.5. Many analysts ignore the option of labeling their measurement levels. Ordinal and nominal labels show up with other icons, namely, as bar charts and Venn diagrams (concentric circles), and an older, but still recent version of SPSS uses a "#" symbol (shown in Screen W17.11) for numeric variables. Again, these are just user-assigned labels that have no effect on our ability to use any statistical procedure later.

Return now to the Data View screen, where variablx is displayed. Place the cursor on variablx, and view the drop-down label defining the variable. The next step is to enter values for variablx. Enter the data from Chapter 6 in the textbook by selecting a data cell, entering a value, and then pressing Enter. (The data are also recorded by simply selecting the keyboard down arrow after entering the numeric data value in each cell.) In this manner, you should reproduce Screen W17.4. You have just completed the data entry for your first variable. Congratulations!

Screen W17.3 ⎯⎯⎯⎯⎯〜⎯ Selecting Variable Type

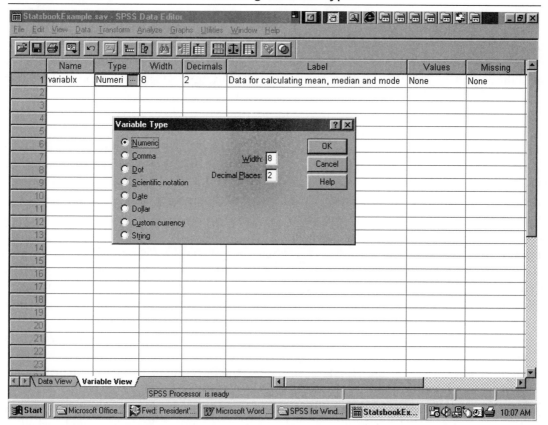

Screen W17.4 ⎯⎯⎯⎯⎯〜⎯ Entering Data

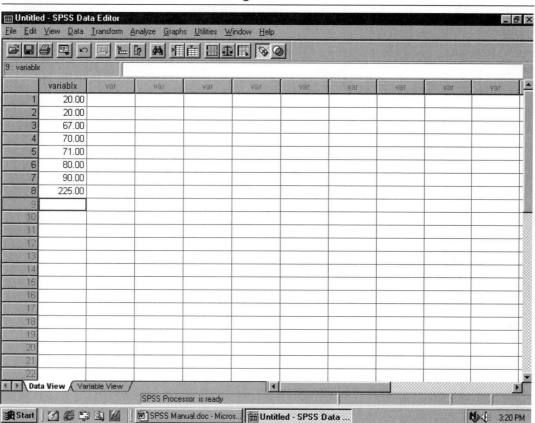

UNIVARIATE ANALYSIS: MEANS AND FREQUENCY DISTRIBUTIONS

You are now ready to perform your first SPSS data analysis. From the toolbar, select Analyze → Descriptive Statistics → Frequencies, which produces the dialog box seen in Screen W17.5. Select variablx and then select the center arrow to move variablx to the Variable(s) box. Next, select the Statistics . . . button at the bottom of the dialog box. This action produces another dialog box, from which you can now select Mean, Median, and Mode, as shown by the checkmarks in Screen W17.6. Then select Continue.

You can also select other analyses. From the Frequency dialog box, select Charts . . . → Histograms → With normal curve, shown in Screen W17.7. Now select Continue to proceed.

After you return to the Frequencies screen, select OK in the Frequencies dialog box. SPSS will then perform the commands you just specified. Screen W17.8—called the Output screen (or Output Viewer)—will be produced. The scroll bar on the right-hand edge of the screen can be used to view the entire output.

Specifically, the results shown in Table W17.1 and Figure W17.1 are produced. (*Note:* You can cut and paste these results into a word processing program, which can be useful when preparing reports and slide shows. Table W17.1 and Figure W17.1 were reproduced in this way.) The number of bars is set by default. However, you can also adjust the number of bars shown in the histogram in Figure W17.1 by opening the Chart Editor. You can do this either by placing the cursor over the histogram on the Output screen and double clicking it, or by selecting Edit → SPSS Chart Object → Open. Once you see the Chart Editor dialog box, select Edit → Select X-Axis → Histogram Options: Bin Sizes → Custom. Select, for example, Number of Intervals: 10, and then select Apply, and see how that changes the display. This is shown in Screen W17.9.

If you had created a bar chart rather than a histogram, a separate bar would be created for each value of the variable. To create a bar chart, select Analyze → Descriptive Statistics → Frequencies → Charts: Bar charts. You might want to want to open up the Chart Editor, and then explore options for changing the bar chart.

Next, extend this example in the following way. Chapter 7 in the textbook features a discussion of how boxplots are used to determine whether individual observations are outliers. You might wonder whether the

Screen W17.5 —————— Frequencies Dialog Box

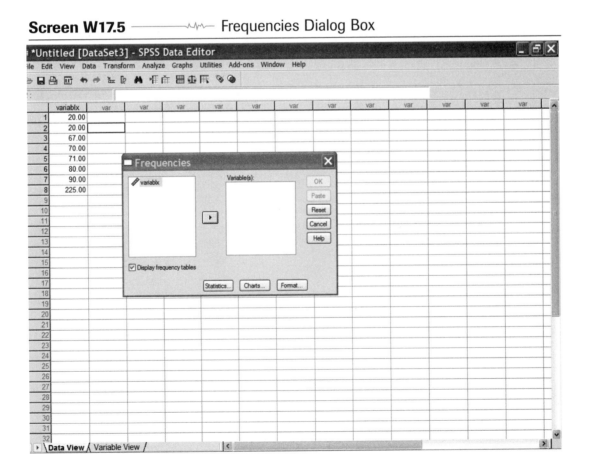

Screen W17.6 ——————— Frequencies: Statistics Dialog Box

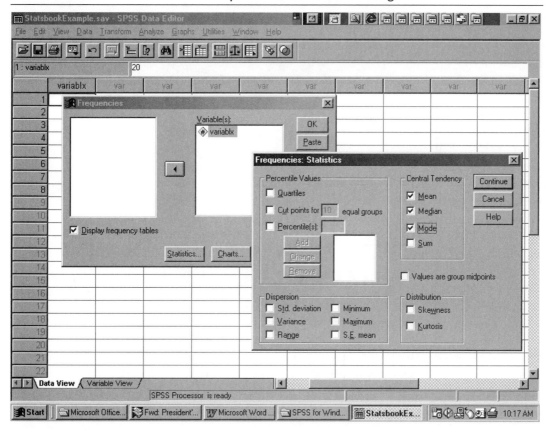

Screen W17.7 ——————— Creating a Histogram

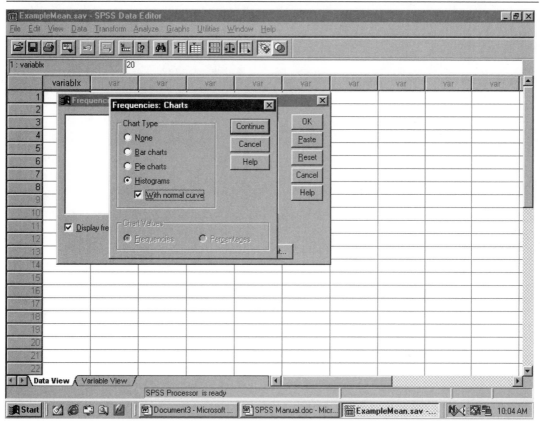

Screen W17.8 ———— ⋀⋁⋀— Output Screen

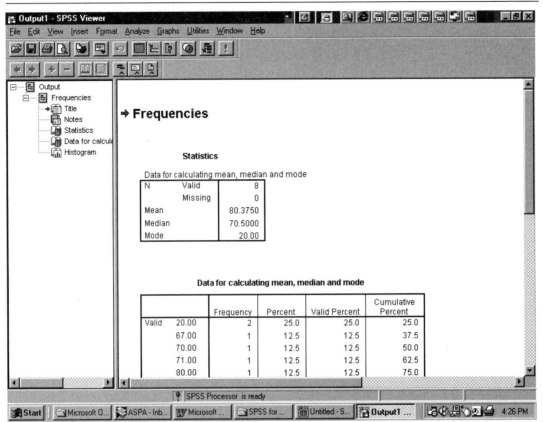

Screen W17.9 ———— ⋀⋁⋀— Chart Editor

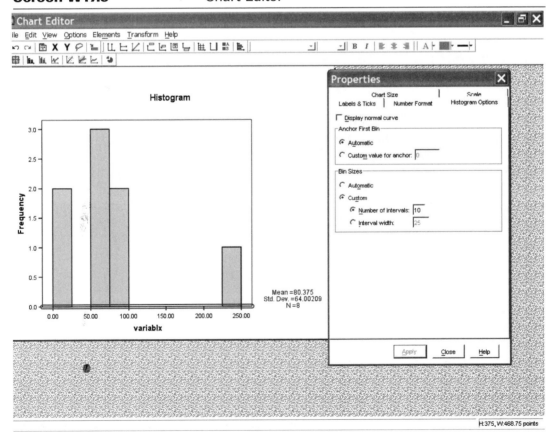

Table W17.1 ———⌁⌁— SPSS Output (in Word Format)

Statistics VARIABLX			
N	Valid	8	
	Missing	0	
Mean		80.3750	
Median		70.5000	
Mode		20.00	

VARIABLX		Frequency	Percent	Valid Percent	Cumulative Percent
Valid	20.00	2	25.0	25.0	25.0
	67.00	1	12.5	12.5	37.5
	70.00	1	12.5	12.5	50.0
	71.00	1	12.5	12.5	62.5
	80.00	1	12.5	12.5	75.0
	90.00	1	12.5	12.5	87.5
	225.00	1	12.5	12.5	100.0
	Total	8	100.0	100.0	

Figure W17.1 ———⌁⌁— Histogram

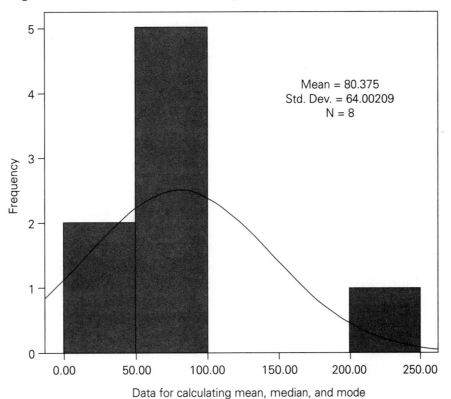

Mean = 80.375
Std. Dev. = 64.00209
N = 8

Data for calculating mean, median, and mode

data point 225 is an outlier, as discussed in the textbook. SPSS can create a boxplot to find out. First, select from the toolbar Graphs → Boxplots. The dialog box shown in Screen W17.10 will appear.

Select Summaries of separate variables → Define. The dialog box shown in Screen W17.11 appears. Select the variable "variablx," and highlight the arrow to the left of the box labeled "Boxes Represent" so that you can drag the variable to the Boxes Represent box. Then, to continue, select OK. The output is produced in the Output screen, as shown in Screen W17.12. Examine the display. Notice that the X-axis depicts the number of cases as being "8." Also note that the eighth observation in the dataset is an outlier. As a part of

Screen W17.10 ———∿∿— Boxplot Dialog Box

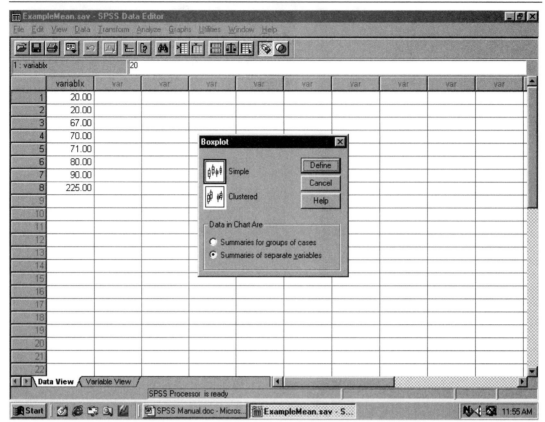

examining a dataset, you should make a note of this observation because it may have an undue influence on further analyses. In this example, there are no observations with small values.

In SPSS, the same output can often be produced in different ways. For example, to produce the boxplot shown in Screen W17.12, you could have used Analyze → Explore → Variable: variablx → OK. No one way is better than any other; both result in the same output. Just choose whatever method works best for you.

To close the Output screen, select File → Close. At this point there is no need to save the output, so select No when asked if you would like to save it, and then return to the Data View screen. However, we will want to save this example dataset as "Example" because we will use it later to develop additional examples and SPSS demonstrations. To save the dataset, use File → Save As → File Name: Example → Save. Be sure to note in which hard disk directory or portable memory device you are saving the file, so that you can find it again.

VARIABLE LABELS AND VALUES

Open the Public Perceptions dataset, which can found on the CD that accompanies this workbook, and be sure you are in the Data View screen. SPSS can show the data both as numbers and as value labels. If you see all labels, as in Screen W17.13, you might want to see the coded numbers instead. To do so, select View → Value Labels. When you see value labels, the Value Labels option has been selected, as shown in Screen W17.13. (Note the check mark next to Value Labels.) To view numbers, simply click on Value Labels to switch off this option (the check mark will disappear). Then the fields will show numbers.

You can also view the value labels in the Variable View screen. In the Variable View screen, select the cell in the Values column that corresponds, for example, with the variable "control." Click on that cell and double click on the square icon that appears in the cell, which will generate the dialog box shown in Screen W17.14. This box defines the values that correspond with the labels "Very Important," "Important,"

Screen W17.11 ————— Defining Boxplot Variables

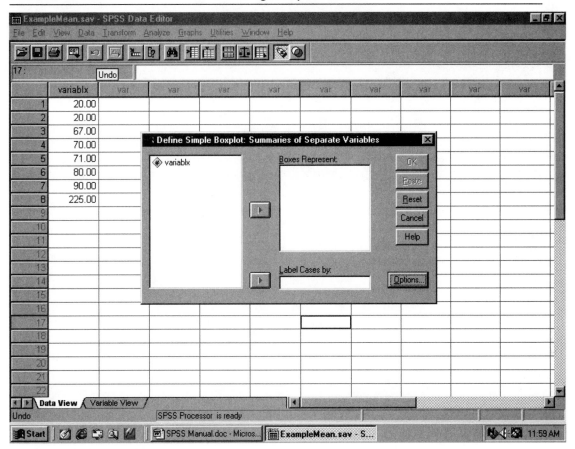

Screen W17.12 ————— Boxplot Output Screen

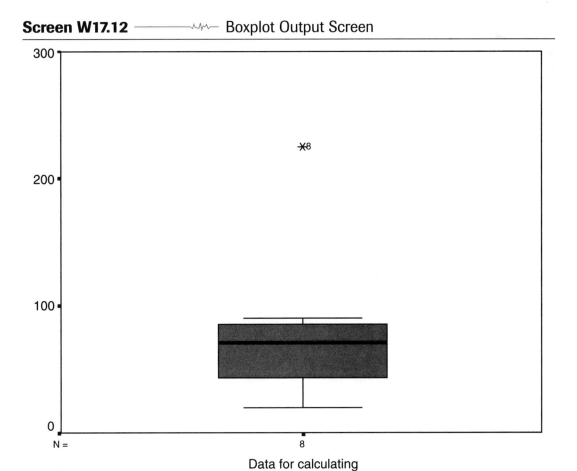

Data for calculating

Screen W17.13 ———⁓⁓— Value Labels

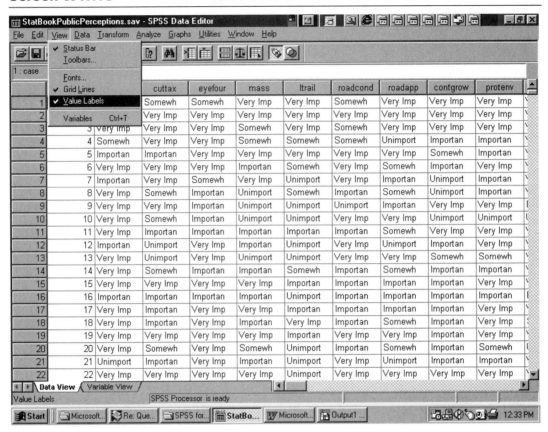

"Somewhat Important," and "Unimportant." Often, you will want to assign values to a variable. For example, on a scale of 1–4, a 1 might indicate that a respondent is "very satisfied" regarding some survey question. Such labels later appear on your output, as well, greatly improving presentation.

Note: Students using the *Public Perceptions—Exercising Essential Statistics* dataset created for use with the *SPSS Student Version* software will notice a slight difference with regard to screen W17.13: row 23 will show the variable "busneeds" rather than "arts." This difference reflects the omission of some variables (such as "pubsafe") from the full Public Perceptions dataset in order to accommodate the restrictions of the *SPSS Student Version* software described on the accompanying CD. However, none of these omitted variables are relevant to any material in this workbook, including this chapter.

Now you should practice generating value labels on your old practice dataset, Example. Assigning labels is quite simple. Open the Example dataset you built earlier. The screen shown in Screen W17.15 should be displayed. Select the Variable View screen. First, create a new variable with which you will practice. In row 2 of the Name column, type "dataskil," which is the name of your variable, shown in Screen W17.16. In the Label column, type "Importance of data analysis skills." This variable represents a hypothetical question posed to public sector managers concerning the importance of data analysis skills. (Double clicking on the Label data box allows label entry and editing of entries.)

Now define data values. Select the box in the Values column data cell for the variable "dataskil." Enter "1" in the Value box and then "Very Important" in the Value Label box. The dialog box should now look as in Screen W17.16. Select Add. This causes the definition to be entered into SPSS programming. After you select Add, Screen W17.17 should appear. Repeat this process. Define the scale values "Important," "Somewhat Important," and Unimportant," which results in Screen W17.18. Select OK to complete the value definitions for this variable. All that remains is for the researcher to enter the data for this hypothetical question.

Screen W17.14 ————— ∿∿∿— Value Labels Dialog Box

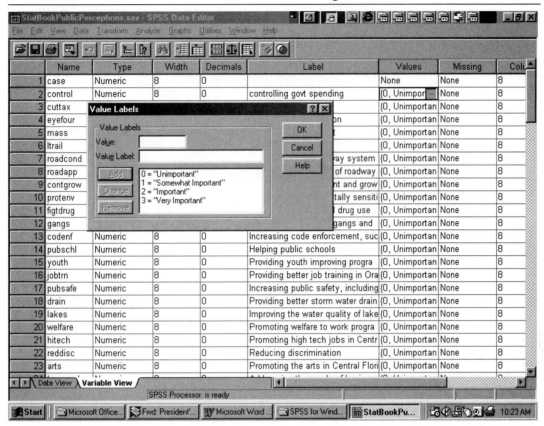

Screen W17.15 ————— ∿∿∿— Generating Labels

Screen W17.16 ———————— Defining Data Values

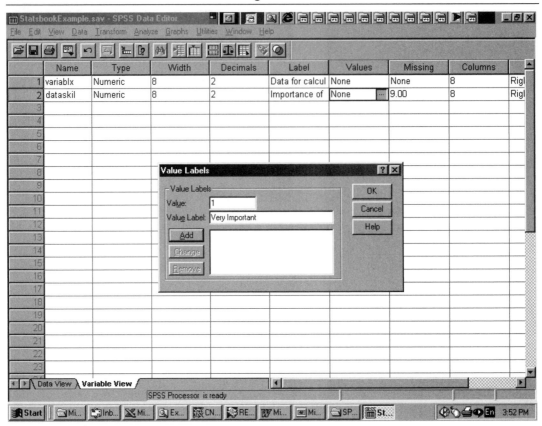

Screen W17.17 ———————— Adding Labels

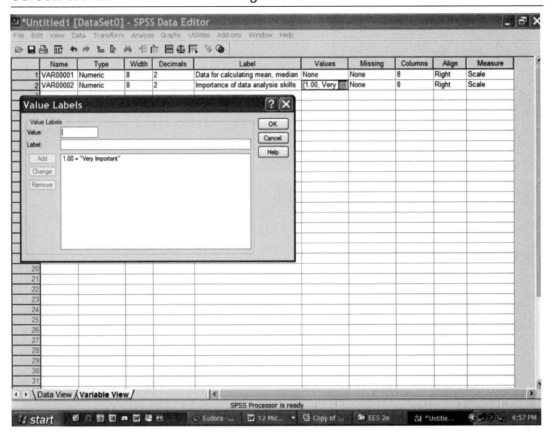

Screen W17.18 ——————〰〰—— Value Label Definitions

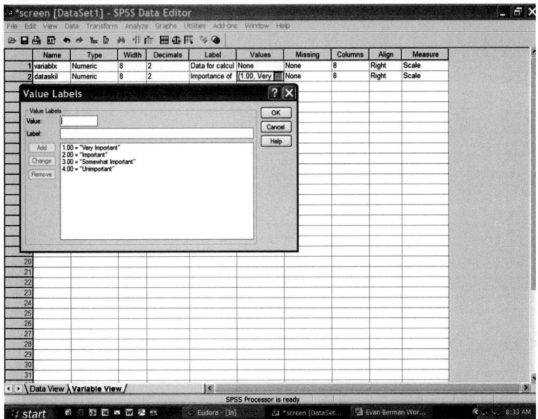

DEFINING MISSING VALUES

A common problem is the coding and handling of missing values. Missing values are blank cells in the Data View screen when an observation has a missing value for a specific variable. Sometimes, however, analysts want to assign a specific value for missing values. Doing so helps differentiate between a value that an analyst has forgotten to enter and a value that really is missing, which occurs when a respondent does not answer a particular question. Suppose you wish to assign the value of "9" as our way of coding missing values. Select the Variable View screen, and highlight the cell in the second row of the "Missing" column. Screen W17.19 will be displayed. Next, select Discrete missing values, and enter a "9" in the first block, and then select OK. This will cause every "9" for the given variable (in this case, dataskil) to be treated as missing. Proper definition of missing data is extremely important to ensure accurate data analysis.

Screen W17.20 shows another highly useful feature of SPSS. Variable definitions (for example, missing values, data values, or labels) are readily copied from one variable to a range of other variables. Thus, you need to define missing values and data values (labels) only once. Indeed, after you create more new variables, newvar1 through newvar5, as shown in Screen W17.20, simply copy and paste the Values definition of the variable "dataskil" to these new cells. You do not need to define these values for each new variable. Similarly, you can now copy and paste the missing values definition from the variable "dataskil" to these new variables, too.

SELECTING A SUBSET OF OBSERVATIONS FOR ANALYSIS

Often, analysts want to perform their analyses on a subset of observations. Using the Public Perceptions dataset, assume that you wish to assess perceptions of client satisfaction, but *only* among those respondents who have had contact with a county employee during the past year. Then, you would want to select for subsequent analysis only those observations that meet this condition.

Screen W17.19 —————∿∿— Missing Values Dialog Box

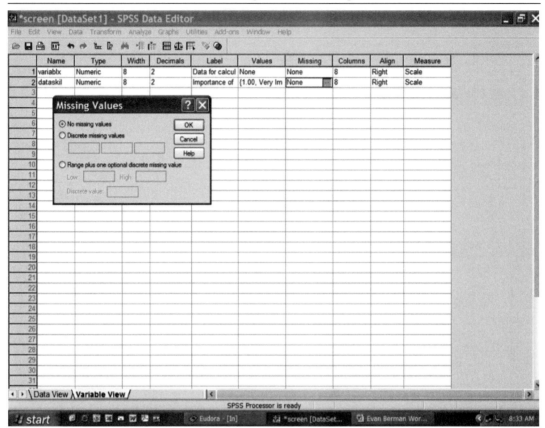

Screen W17.20 —————∿∿— Copying Variable Definitions

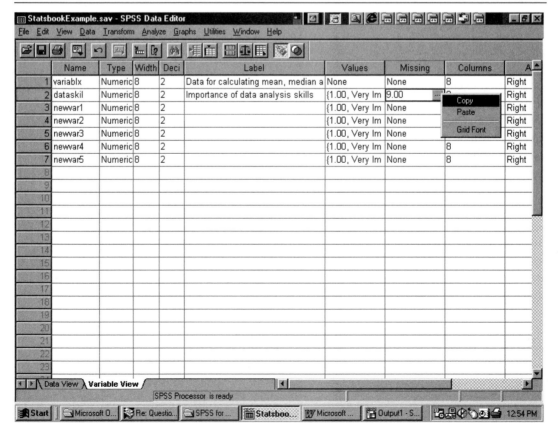

Screen W17.21 ——————— ∿∿— Selecting Cases (Filtering Observations)

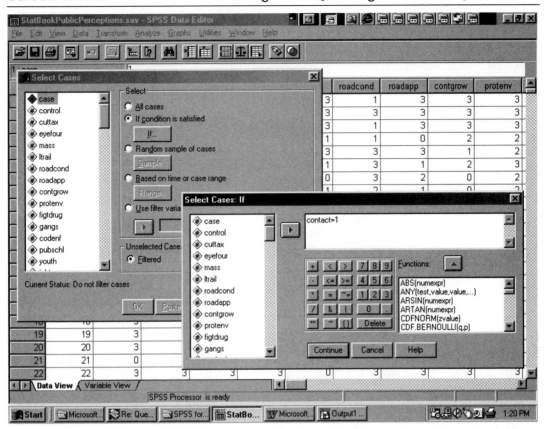

Open the Public Perceptions dataset. The variable "contact" (row 29) measures whether the respondent has had contact with county employees within the past year. To filter out respondents not meeting this criterion, perform the following sequence of commands. From the toolbar, select Data → Select Cases → If condition is satisfied. Add "contact" to the right-hand box, and type "=1". Screen W17.21 is displayed. Select Continue → OK. Note the left-hand column of the Data View screen. Observations not meeting our new requirement of having contact with county employees during the past year now show a diagonal line through their respective sequence number, indicating that they are not included in subsequent calculations (Screen W17.22). (To undo this restriction, simply choose Data → Select Cases → Select: All cases → OK.)

INDEX VARIABLES I: CRONBACH ALPHA

Chapter 3 of the textbook discusses the use of index variables to measure concepts comprised of several dimensions. In short, different variables are used to measure different dimensions, and these variables are subsequently aggregated into an index variable.

Remember, index variable construction is a two-step process. Before aggregating the data, you need to *justify* (that is, to persuasively argue) that the disparate variables indeed measure different dimensions of the same underlying concept (see Chapter 3 of the textbook). The justification should be based on theoretical grounds (do the variables make sense as dimensions of the same underlying concept?) and empirical grounds. One way to empirically justify the selection of variables is to examine the extent to which the disparate variables are correlated with each other. If the variables measure dimensions of the *same* concept, then the dimensions should be correlated with each other, as well.

Cronbach alpha is the measure that assesses the empirical correlation (or internal reliability) of variables. As discussed in Chapter 3, values between 0.80 and 1.00 indicate high internal reliability, and values between 0.70 and 0.80 indicate moderate but acceptable internal reliability.

Screen W17.22 ———— ⋀⋁⋀ — Selected Cases

	case	control	cuttax	eyefour	mass	ltrail	roadcond	roadapp	contgrow	protenv
1	1	2	1	1	3	3	1	3	3	3
2	2	3	3	3	3	3	3	3	3	3
3	3	3	3	3	1	3	1	3	3	3
4	4	1	3	3	1	1	1	0	2	2
5	5	2	2	3	3	3	3	3	1	2
6	6	3	3	3	2	1	3	1	2	3
7	7	2	3	1	3	0	3	2	0	2
8	8	3	1	2	0	1	2	1	0	2
9	9	3	3	2	0	0	0	2	3	3
10	10	3	1	2	0	0	3	3	0	0
11	11	3	2	2	2	2	2	1	3	3
12	12	2	0	3	2	0	3	0	2	3
13	13	3	0	3	0	0	3	3	1	1
14	14	3	1	2	2	1	2	1	2	2
15	15	3	3	3	3	2	2	2	2	3
16	16	2	2	2	2	0	2	2	2	2
17	17	3	2	3	3	2	2	2	2	3
18	18	3	2	3	2	3	2	1	2	3
19	19	3	3	3	3	2	3	3	2	3
20	20	3	1	3	1	0	2	1	2	1
21	21	0	2	3	2	0	3	0	2	2
22	22	3	3	3	3	0	3	3	3	3

Open the Public Perceptions dataset. This dataset contains several variables (survey items) that can be used to measure customer satisfaction. Specifically, go to the Variable View screen. Scroll down to the first of these variables, helpful (on or about row 32). Double click on the Label cell; this allows you to scroll the entire label entry ("the employees were helpful"). The other variables—respect, friendly, nomistak, and exceed—are immediately below that variable. These individual variables appear to be possible dimensions of an overall concept, for example, "customer satisfaction." Screen W17.23 also shows the value labels for these items (rows 32 through 37).

Next, examine the Cronbach alpha statistic to determine whether these items are adequately correlated with each other. But first, practice what you learned in the previous section; you wish to create the index variable only for respondents who have had contact with county officials in the past year. Select only those observations that meet this condition, that is, "contact=1." This selection produces a screen similar to Screen W17.21.

The command sequence for producing the Cronbach alpha statistic is Analyze → Scale → Reliability Analysis. Add all six variables to the Items box. Then, select Statistics and, from the "Descriptives for" box, the items "Item," "Scale," "Scale if item deleted," as shown in Screen W17.24. Then, to perform the analysis, select Continue and OK. Screen W17.25 shows the results. Note that the value for alpha is .8825. This value is well within the required range of 0.8 to 1.0, indicating a very high degree of *internal consistency* (or *internal reliability*). Also note that deleting any item (variable), as shown in the right-hand column, results in a lower value for alpha. Therefore, combining these separate dimension variables into a concept index variable, "customer satisfaction," is empirically justified. Finally, note that the number of observations is now limited to 353, reflecting both the constraint (contact=1) and missing values for some of the six variables. (If the analysis had not been limited to only those respondents who have had contact, the result would have been $n = 615$ and alpha = .8855, resulting in the same conclusion.)

Screen W17.23 ───────〰〰─ Value Labels for Public Perceptions Dataset

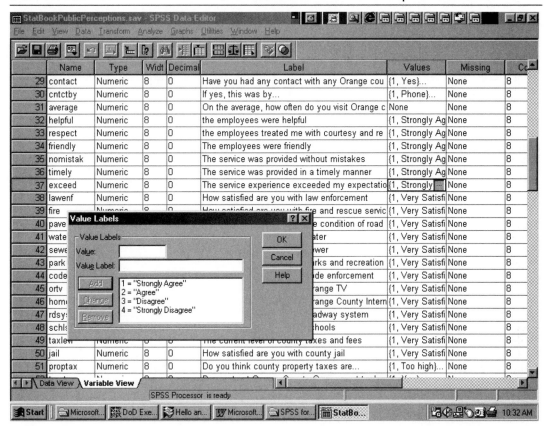

Screen W17.24 ───────〰〰─ Producing Cronbach Alpha

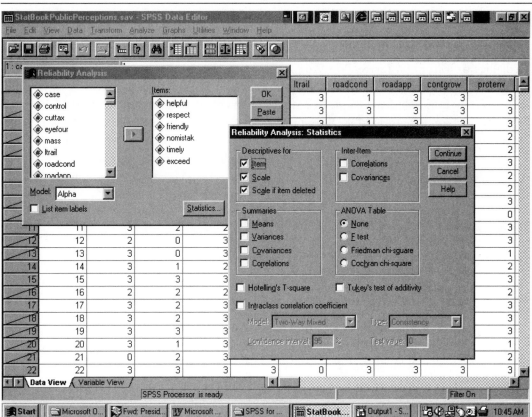

Screen W17.25 ————— ⋀⋀⋁⋀ Cronbach Alpha Output

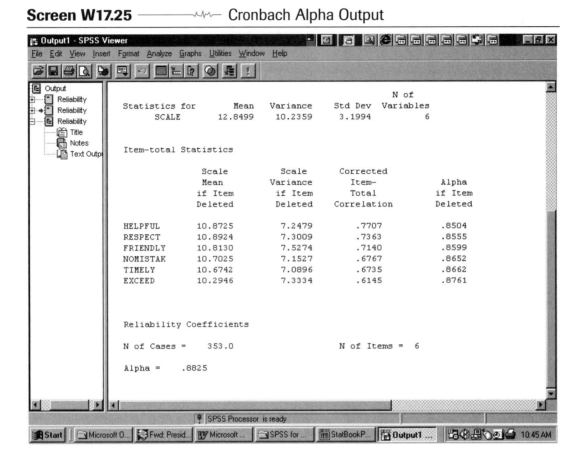

INDEX VARIABLES II: CONSTRUCTION

Now you will construct the index variable. From the toolbar, select Transform → Compute. The Compute Variable dialog box will appear (Screen W17.26). In the Target Variable box, enter the name of your new index variable for customer satisfaction, satisfyd. In the Numeric Expression box, enter the six variables comprising your index variable, and divide by six. Be sure to note the brackets in Screen W17.25 to ensure the appropriate division. Then select OK. Examine the Data View screen; satisfyd is now the last variable. Examine the new variable using Analyze → Descriptive Statistics → Frequencies, which yields the results shown in Screen W17.27. Also, you can produce summary statistics by selecting Frequencies → Statistics; choose Mean, Median, and Mode from the Central Tendency box, and then select Continue → OK.

RECODING DATA

Depending on a variable's data distribution, there may be so many response categories and resulting low frequency counts that recoding the variable is not only appropriate but will also allow for more meaningful data interpretation. Redefining data into new categories is a relatively simple process.

Open the Public Perceptions dataset. Perform a frequency distribution and histogram of the variable "ethnic." The output shown in Screen W17.28 and Figure W17.2 is produced. (Be sure to select all cases for this analysis.) You will see that "ethnic" has several response categories with low counts. Asian/Pacific Islander (category 4), Native American (5), and Other (6) could be reasonably redefined as an aggregate variable "Other." Doing so would yield a total of four categories within the variable "ethnic." Specifically, the new variable, "ethrecod," will have the following categories: 1 = White, 2 = Black/African-American, 3 = Hispanic, and 4 = Other.

Screen W17.26 ———~/~— Constructing the Index Variable for "Customer Satisfaction"

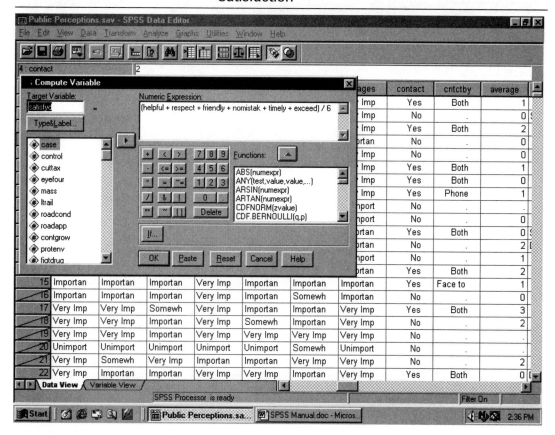

Screen W17.27 ———~/~— Output Screen for Satisfyd

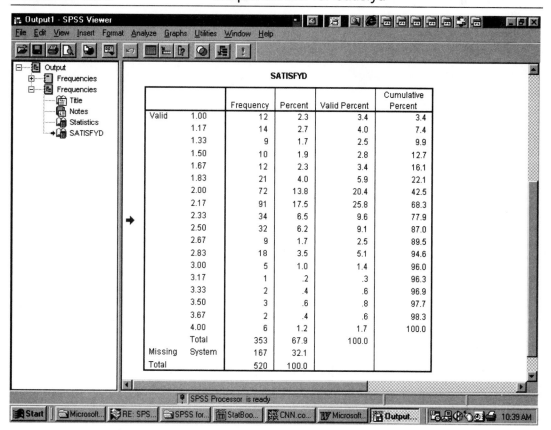

SATISFYD

		Frequency	Percent	Valid Percent	Cumulative Percent
Valid	1.00	12	2.3	3.4	3.4
	1.17	14	2.7	4.0	7.4
	1.33	9	1.7	2.5	9.9
	1.50	10	1.9	2.8	12.7
	1.67	12	2.3	3.4	16.1
	1.83	21	4.0	5.9	22.1
	2.00	72	13.8	20.4	42.5
	2.17	91	17.5	25.8	68.3
	2.33	34	6.5	9.6	77.9
	2.50	32	6.2	9.1	87.0
	2.67	9	1.7	2.5	89.5
	2.83	18	3.5	5.1	94.6
	3.00	5	1.0	1.4	96.0
	3.17	1	.2	.3	96.3
	3.33	2	.4	.6	96.9
	3.50	3	.6	.8	97.7
	3.67	2	.4	.6	98.3
	4.00	6	1.2	1.7	100.0
	Total	353	67.9	100.0	
Missing	System	167	32.1		
Total		520	100.0		

Screen W17.28 ————〰— Output Screen for Ethnic

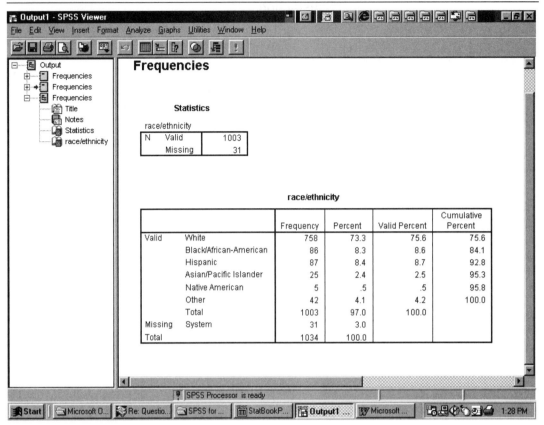

Figure W17.2————〰—Race/Ethnicity Output

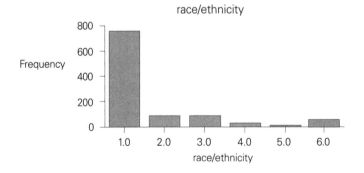

To perform recoding, you will recode and create a new variable, "ethrecod," in order to preserve the coding of the existing variable. Select Transform → Recode → Into Different Variables. Then select the existing variable, "ethnic," which results in the dialog box shown in Screen W17.29. Note that the dialog box is now prompting the user for the name of the new variable (note the question mark in the dialog box). Type "ethrecod" in the Name box, shown in Screen W17.30. Next, select Change (in the far right of the dialog box) to complete this part of the variable recoding, which should produce Screen W17.31.

Now that you have defined the new variable, you must define the new categories. Select Old and New Values, which brings up the dialog box shown in Screen W17.32. The original values for response categories 1 should be retained. Enter "1" for both Old Value and New Value, and then Add. In turn, Screens W17.33 and W17.34 are produced.

Continue this procedure for response categories 2 and 3. Now recode response categories 4, 5, and 6 into a single new category, 4. Select Range, and enter "4" and "6". Note that the New Value cell is now illuminated; enter "4" → Add. To ensure that missing data from the original variable are retained and recog-

Screen W17.29 ———— ∿∿ — Recoding Values for Ethnic

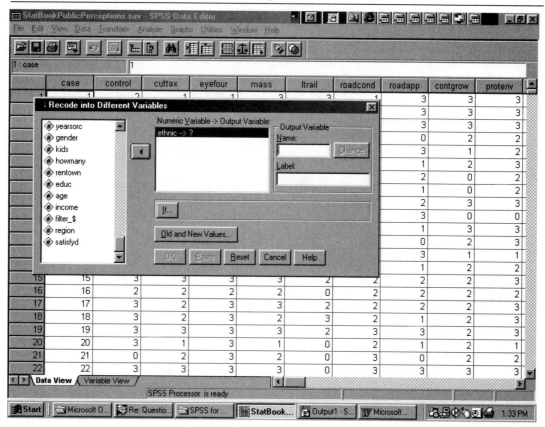

Screen W17.30 ———— ∿∿ — Naming the Variable

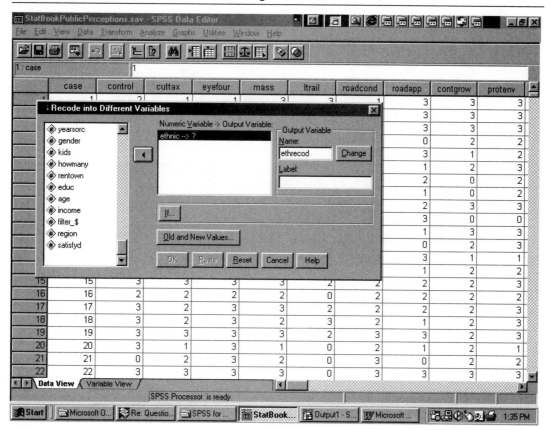

Screen W17.31 ————— 〰️〰️〰️ ——— Recoding Dialog Box

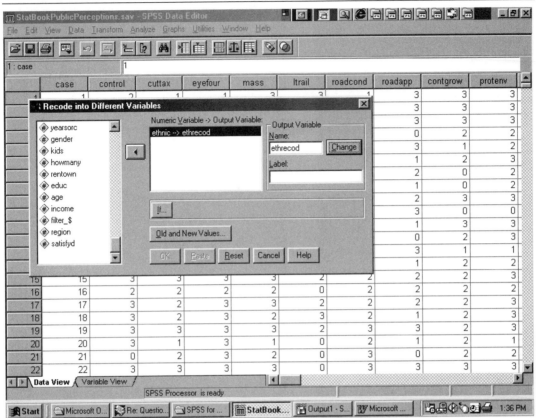

Screen W17.32 ————— 〰️〰️〰️ ——— Old and New Values

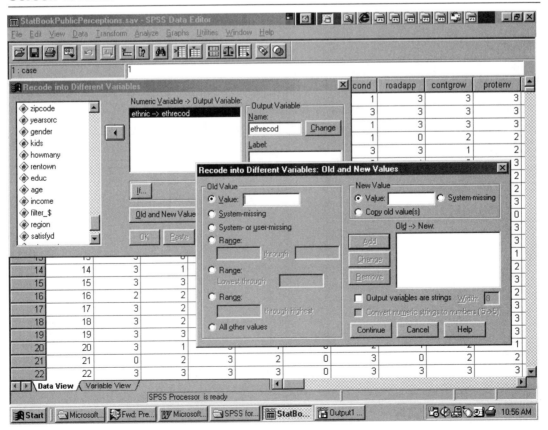

Screen W17.33 ———————〰〰— Entering New Value

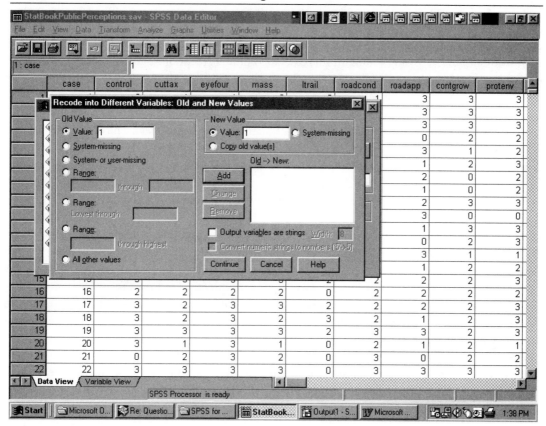

Screen W17.34 ———————〰〰— Old to New Values

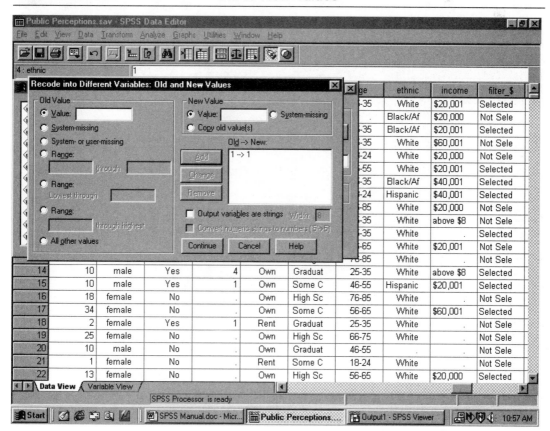

nized as such by SPSS, select "System- or user-missing" under Old Value, and "System-missing" under New Value → Add. Screen W17.35 is displayed. As an important side note, observe the two cells "System-or user-missing" and "System-missing." System-missing cells are empty, whereas user-missing cells have user-defined missing values, as discussed earlier. It is a safe practice to specify System- or user-missing when the intent is to refer to all missing values. In this case, the Public Perceptions dataset does not contain user-defined missing values (verify this in the Variable View screen, Missing column); thus, using System-missing and System- or user-missing produces the same result.

Select Continue and OK to complete the recoding. To verify that the recoding was successful, perform a Frequency Distribution (recall, Analyze → Descriptive Statistics → Frequencies). The output shown in Screen W17.36 and Figure W17.3 are displayed. The total number of valid responses is still 1,003; there are still 31 missing system values; and the total number of responses is still 1,034. Also, the number of responses comprising the new value of 4 is 72, the sum of Old Values (prior to recoding) of categories 4, 5, and 6. To finish construction of the new variable, "ethrecod," remember to define Values and Label on the Variable View screen.

The same procedure is used to define a response value *within* a variable as missing. For example, from the Public Perceptions dataset, select the variable "trust." This variable has three response categories, "Yes," "No," and "Can't Say." To recode "Can't Say" as a missing value, select Transform → Recode → Into Same Variable. When defining response category 3, enter "3" under Old Value and then select "System-missing" for the New Value. The dialog box shown in Screen W17.37 should be displayed. Select Continue to complete the recoding. Examine the variable "trust." Previous cells containing a "Can't Say" response are now coded as missing, as indicated by a period.

Another use for recoding might be to combine response categories from scales, possibly when cell counts are less than sufficient for evaluation. For example, a seven-point Likert scale might have the following response categories: "Strongly Agree," "Agree," "Somewhat Agree," "Neutral," "Somewhat Disagree,"

Screen W17.35 ———〰〰— Missing Data Screen

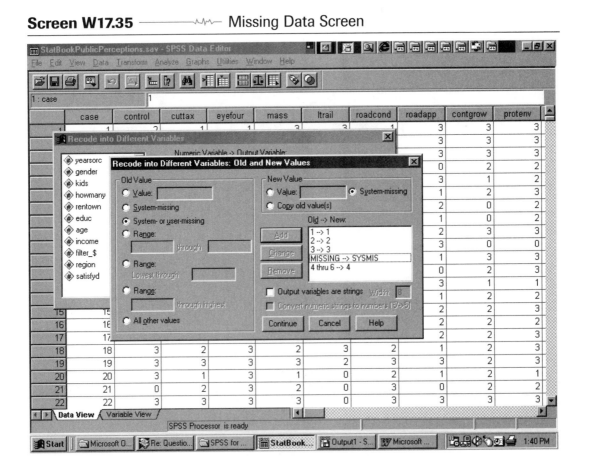

Screen W17.36 ————— ⟶⟿⟿— Output for Recoded Data

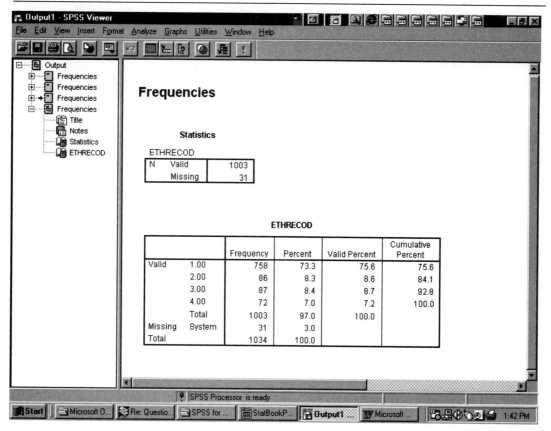

Figure W17.3 ————— ⟶⟿⟿— Recoded Data Bar Chart

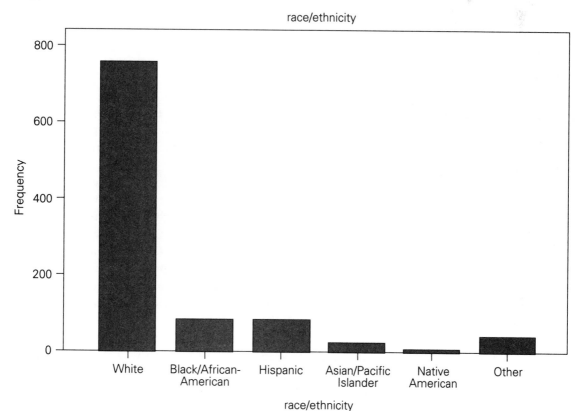

Screen W17.37 ———⟋⋏⋏⋎— Recoding Response as a Missing Category

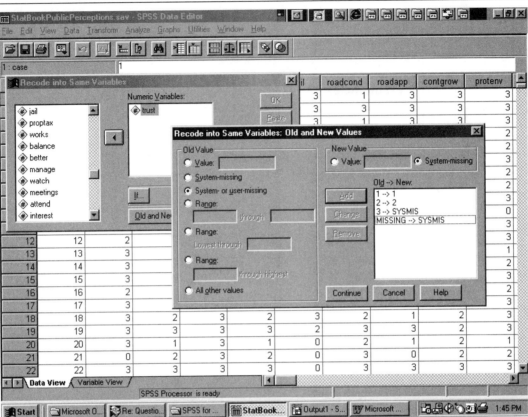

"Disagree," and "Strongly Disagree." This scale could be easily recoded to five response categories by recoding "Strongly Agree/Agree" to "Agree," and "Strongly Disagree/Disagree" to "Disagree."

HYPOTHESIS TESTING WITH CHI-SQUARE

In Chapter 8 of the textbook, you learned that a *contingency table* expresses the relationship between two categorical variables. One variable is shown in rows and the other in columns. Each row shows the frequency of observations with specific values for both variables. Typically, column totals are present. Statistics such as chi-square express the relationship between variables quantitatively. SPSS easily performs contingency table analysis.

Open the Public Perceptions dataset. In the Variable View screen, highlight the variable "interest." The variable label identifies that this variable assesses the extent to which respondents feel county government is interested in what they have to say about issues affecting them. An analyst might ask whether a significant difference exists between the opinions held by male and female respondents on this question.

Chapter 9 of the textbook discusses the concept of the null hypothesis and its application in hypothesis testing. For this exercise, the null hypothesis (H_0) is "Gender has no effect on perception of government interest in citizen opinions." The alternative hypothesis (H_A) is "Gender does influence perceptions of government interest in citizen opinions." You now want to examine whether sufficient statistical evidence exists to reject the null hypothesis and, hence, establish that a relationship does exist. To test this hypothesis, select Analyze → Descriptive Statistics → Crosstabs. Then select "gender" in the column and "interest" in rows. Also, select Statistics → Chi-square → Continue. The dialog box shown in Screen W17.38 will be displayed. Note how the selection of "gender" in the column is consistent with Chapter 9 in the textbook.

Next, select Cells → Observed → Column → Total → Continue → OK. The results in Figure W17.4 will be produced. First, note that 443 males and 551 females make up the total sample. Second, note the

Screen W17.38 ———— ⌇⌇⌇ —— Chi-Square Dialog Box

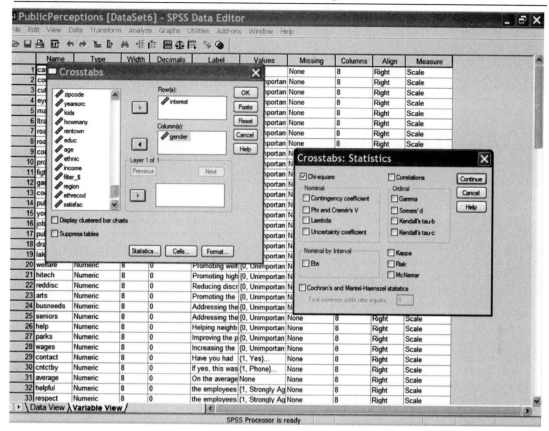

Figure W17.4 ———— ⌇⌇⌇ —— Chi-Square Output

I believe that the county government is interested in what I have to say about issues that affect me. *gender Crosstabulation

			gender		Total
			male	female	
I believe that the county government is interested in what I have to say about issues that affect me.	Strongly Agree	Count % within gender	11 2.5%	19 3.4%	30 3.0%
	Agree	Count % within gender	236 53.3%	326 59.2%	562 56.5%
	Disagree	Count % within gender	153 34.5%	171 31.0%	324 32.6%
	Strongly Disagree	Count % within gender	43 9.7%	35 6.4%	78 7.8%
Total		Count % within gender	443 100.0%	551 100.0%	994 100.0%

Chi-Square Tests

	Value	df	Asymp. Sig. (2-sided)
Pearson Chi-Square	6.711[a]	3	.082
Likelihood Ratio	6.699	3	.082
Linear-by-Linear Association	6.590	1	.010
N of Valid Cases	944		

a. 0 cells (.0%) have expected count less than 5. The minimum expected count is 13.37

Screen W17.39 ——— ⎯⋀⋀⎯ Output Screen for T-Test

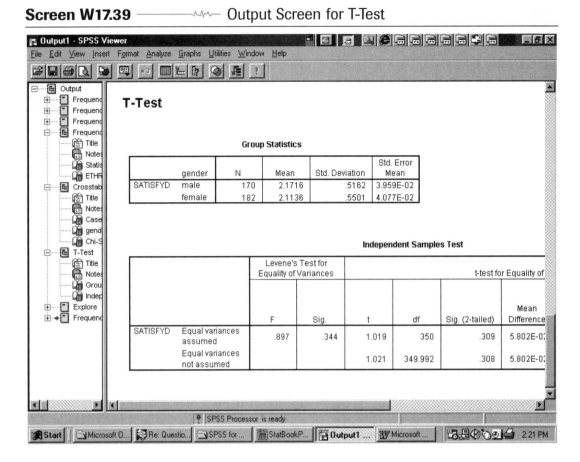

percentages produced within columns. These indicate how males and females responded to this question. For example, 34.5 percent of males and 31.0 percent of females disagree that county government is interested in what they have to say about issues affecting them.

Review the remaining response categories. Is there a significant difference between male and female respondents? To answer that question, you should rely on the chi-square calculation, which produces the results also shown in Figure W17.4. The chi-square value 6.711 is significant at the 0.082 level. Since this value exceeds the 0.05 standard for statistical significance, you cannot reject the null hypothesis, which means that there is insufficient statistical evidence to conclude that a relationship exists between gender and interest shown by county officials in issues that affect respondents.

T-TESTS

Chapter 11 of the textbook discusses how t-tests are used to determine whether two groups have different means of a continuous variable. For example, do men and women differ in their opinion of the quality of service they receive from county employees? If there is a perceived difference, perhaps county employees deal differently with male and female residents. Again, you need to limit the analysis to those respondents who have had contact with county employees (that is, if contact = 1; see "Selecting a Subset of Observations for Analysis," above).

The null hypothesis (H_0) in this case is "Men and women do not have different opinions of the quality of service they receive from county employees." The alternate hypothesis (H_A) is "Men and women do have different opinions of the quality of service they receive from county employees."

Open the Public Perceptions dataset. Select Analyze → Compare Means → Independent Samples T-Test. Screen W17.39 will be displayed. Enter "satisfyd" in the Test Variable box and gender in the Group-

Screen W17.40 ───────〰〰─── Independent Samples T-Test Dialog Box

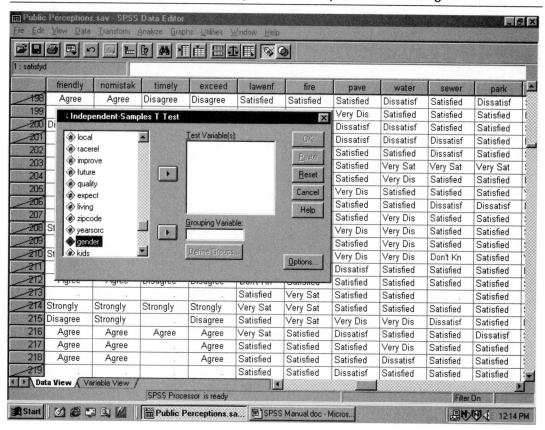

ing Variable box. SPSS requires definition of the dichotomous values of "gender" that constitute the grouping variable. Enter "1" and "2" for Group 1 and Group 2, respectively. (When the grouping variable is continuous, a cutoff point—called "Cut Point" in Screen W17.40—is specified, which creates the two groups.)

Select Continue → OK. The output shown in Screen W17.41 is produced. The results show that the mean level of satisfaction is 2.17 among men and 2.11 among women. The statistical question is whether this difference in the survey sample is large enough to suggest that a difference exists in the population of all county residents, as well.

As discussed in Chapter 11 of the textbook, using a t-test is a two-step process. First, we test whether the variances of the two groups are equal. The null hypothesis is that variances are equal. According to the output shown in Screen W17.41, you cannot reject this null hypothesis ($p = .344$). Second, you will test whether the difference of means (2.17 versus 2.11) is statistically significant. The result of this t-test is 1.019, which is significant at $p = .309$. This value exceeds the standard of 5 percent; thus, you conclude that in the population of all county residents, no statistically significant difference exists between men and women with regard to this item. (You also could have examined certain assumptions of the t-test, such as whether the variable is normally distributed and whether any extreme values are present that might affect the analysis.)

CONCLUSION

By now, you have seen just how valuable a tool statistical software can be to public managers and policy analysts. In particular, SPSS's user-friendly package can make statistics easier and save valuable time by "doing the math." Instead of struggling through cumbersome equations, analysts can quickly assess their data and present their findings. In short, analysts now readily recognize the importance of statistical software packages such as SPSS in helping them to quickly add value to decision-making processes.

Screen W17.41 ———— ᐯᐯᐯ— Dichotomous Value Dialog Box

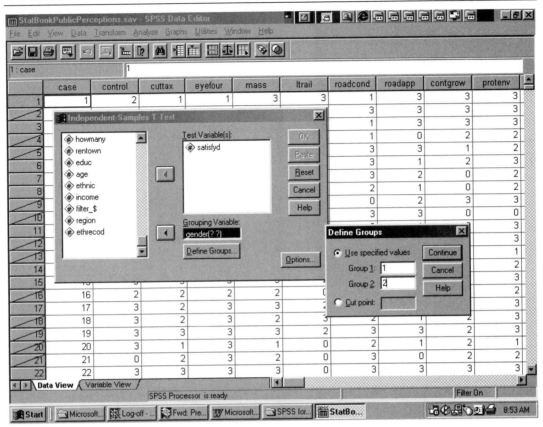

This guide touched on a number of practical statistical applications, but SPSS has many other features, which you can explore on your own. For example, SPSS can be used to merge datasets, which is described on the accompanying CD (see "SPSS Student Version"). SPSS can also produce a wide range of other statistics. After you have familiarized yourself with other statistics described in the textbook, be sure to consult the SPSS manual that comes with your software to learn about other software features and functions.

PUBLIC PERCEPTIONS

General Description

The Public Perceptions dataset includes data from 1,034 telephone interviews among residents of Orange County, Florida. Orange County is the central metropolitan county of Central Florida, encompassing many major tourist attractions. Random digit dialing was used to select interviewees. This is a general citizen survey, encompassing assessments of general county conditions, satisfaction with county services, and demographic items.

As students, some of you may wonder why you should care about these results from Florida. The answer is simple: they could very well have been from your city or county. Such general surveys help managers and policy makers know, in valid ways, where citizens stand on a broad range of issues. Moreover, many citizen surveys explore related questions, and you may be involved in a similar effort or one that is targeted at assessing perceptions about a specific program or service.

Methods

A full description of the survey methods used to develop this dataset is provided in Box 5.1 of the textbook.

Detailed Summary

The survey instrument has seven sections encompassing 96 separate items and is reproduced below. The first section asks the importance of various issues to residents, from controlling government spending to building a light rail transportation system. The rationale for asking these questions is that their ranking may inform county officials in their strategic planning and allocation decisions. The second section asks about perceptions of service experience, generally. Customer service is a key concern to jurisdictions, especially those located close to Disney World, which offers world-class customer service. The third section assesses overall satisfaction with selected county services. The fourth section asks about property taxes. The fifth section addresses a few wide-ranging questions on some matters of current interest to the county. Of particular interest was how often residents watched the local county cable TV station, called Orange TV. The sixth section addresses some general conditions, such as trust in government, expectations of living in Orange County in future years, and perceptions of race relations. Finally, the seventh section provides demographic data regarding age, gender, income, race, and other items. These items are relevant to the analysis of the preceding items. For example, are overall levels of satisfaction with Orange County services associated with perceptions of public safety?

Note on Variables

Each survey item is represented as a variable in the dataset. The variables appear in the same order as in the survey instrument. The variable names are limited to eight characters, and the labels are consistent with the survey items. Variable values are indicated on the survey below, in the first line of each section or as appropriate. Missing values have been coded as periods (.) in the dataset. The sections use a broad range of response scales. The scale on the first section is modified from a seven-point Likert scale. Because all of these items were thought to be of some importance to respondents, a decision was made to group the categories "Very Unimportant," "Unimportant," and "Somewhat Unimportant" in one category labeled "Unimportant."

The survey also includes one continuous variable, the index variable "satisfac." This variable is the average of the six items shown in Survey Question II, which assesses citizen contact with county employees. This variable is provided only for the 353 respondents who have had contact.

Students using *SPSS Student Version* software will find additional information relevant to that software on the CD that accompanies this workbook.

Survey Instrument: Orange County Citizen Survey

Hi, My name is _____, and I'm calling from the Survey Research Laboratory at the University of Central Florida. This is a legitimate survey; I'm not selling anything. We want to know how you feel about several issues facing Orange County. Of course, your participation is completely voluntary, but we hope you will participate. The entire interview should take less than ten minutes. The validity of our results depends on your willingness to help, so we hope that you will participate. Of course, you may discontinue the interview at any time or refuse to answer any questions that make you uncomfortable. We will only report group tendencies in this survey. Your individual answers will be held in strict confidence. Do you have any questions you want to ask before we begin? If you have any questions after the survey, you should call _____, at UCF. His number is 407-xxx-xxxx.

In order for our survey to be valid, we must interview only persons over the age of eighteen living in Orange County. Would that be you?

If "NO," ask to speak to someone who is eligible, and start over or terminate the call.

I. How important are the following issues for you? Please state whether you consider each issue Very Important, Important, Somewhat Important, or Unimportant:

	Very Important	Important	Somewhat Important	Unimportant
Controlling government spending	[3]	[2]	[1]	[0]
Cutting property taxes	[ ]	[ ]	[ ]	[ ]
Reducing I-4 congestion	[ ]	[ ]	[ ]	[ ]
Improving mass transit	[ ]	[ ]	[ ]	[ ]
Building light rail	[ ]	[ ]	[ ]	[ ]
The condition of roadway system	[ ]	[ ]	[ ]	[ ]
Improving the appearance of roadways, such as by burying overhead power lines, reducing the number of billboards, and adding greenery	[ ]	[ ]	[ ]	[ ]
Controlling development and growth	[ ]	[ ]	[ ]	[ ]
Protecting environmentally sensitive land	[ ]	[ ]	[ ]	[ ]
Fighting against illegal drug use	[ ]	[ ]	[ ]	[ ]
Addressing problem of gangs and gang violence, including removing graffiti	[ ]	[ ]	[ ]	[ ]
Increasing code enforcement, such as removing junk and abandoned cars from neighborhoods	[ ]	[ ]	[ ]	[ ]
Helping public schools	[ ]	[ ]	[ ]	[ ]
Providing youth improvement programs, including after-school programs	[ ]	[ ]	[ ]	[ ]

	Very Important	Important	Somewhat Important	Unimportant
Providing better job training in Orange County	[ ]	[ ]	[ ]	[ ]
Increasing public safety, including hiring more deputies	[ ]	[ ]	[ ]	[ ]
Providing better storm water drainage	[ ]	[ ]	[ ]	[ ]
Improving the water quality of lakes	[ ]	[ ]	[ ]	[ ]
Promoting welfare to work programs	[ ]	[ ]	[ ]	[ ]
Promoting high tech jobs in Central Florida	[ ]	[ ]	[ ]	[ ]
Reducing discrimination	[ ]	[ ]	[ ]	[ ]
Promoting the arts in Central Florida	[ ]	[ ]	[ ]	[ ]
Addressing the needs of business	[ ]	[ ]	[ ]	[ ]
Addressing the needs of senior citizens through programs and services	[ ]	[ ]	[ ]	[ ]
Helping neighborhoods	[ ]	[ ]	[ ]	[ ]
Improving the parks	[ ]	[ ]	[ ]	[ ]
Increasing the level of wages	[ ]	[ ]	[ ]	[ ]

II. Have you had contact with any Orange County employees during the past twelve months (not a family member or friend)?

Yes [1]   No [2]

If yes, was this: by phone [1], face-to-face [2], or both [3]? *(Check one.)*
On the average, how often do you visit county offices?_____ (number)

Thinking about those experiences, or your most recent contact with a County employee, please tell me whether you Strongly Agree, Agree, Disagree, or Strongly Disagree with the following statements:

	Strongly Agree	Agree	Disagree	Strongly Disagree
The employees were helpful.	[1]	[2]	[3]	[4]
The employees treated me with courtesy and respect.	[ ]	[ ]	[ ]	[ ]
The employees were friendly.	[ ]	[ ]	[ ]	[ ]
The service was provided without mistakes.	[ ]	[ ]	[ ]	[ ]
The service experience exceeded my expectations.	[ ]	[ ]	[ ]	[ ]
The service was provided in a timely manner.	[ ]	[ ]	[ ]	[ ]

III. How satisfied are you with the following services in Orange County? Would you say you are Very Satisfied, Satisfied, Dissatisfied, or Very Dissatisfied?

	Very Satisfied	Satisfied	Don't Know	Dissatisfied	Very Dissatisfied
Law enforcement	[1]	[2]	[3]	[4]	[5]
Fire and rescue services	[ ]	[ ]	[ ]	[ ]	[ ]
The condition of road pavement	[ ]	[ ]	[ ]	[ ]	[ ]
Water	[ ]	[ ]	[ ]	[ ]	[ ]
Sewer	[ ]	[ ]	[ ]	[ ]	[ ]
Parks and recreation	[ ]	[ ]	[ ]	[ ]	[ ]
Code enforcement	[ ]	[ ]	[ ]	[ ]	[ ]
Orange TV	[ ]	[ ]	[ ]	[ ]	[ ]
Orange County Internet homepage	[ ]	[ ]	[ ]	[ ]	[ ]
Roadway system	[ ]	[ ]	[ ]	[ ]	[ ]
Schools	[ ]	[ ]	[ ]	[ ]	[ ]
The current level of county taxes and fees	[ ]	[ ]	[ ]	[ ]	[ ]
County jail	[ ]	[ ]	[ ]	[ ]	[ ]

IV. Do you think county property taxes are:

Too high	[1]
Too low	[2]
Just about right	[3]
Don't know	[4]

V. The following questions can be answered with a simple yes or no.

Do you trust Orange County Government to do what is right most of the time?
    Yes [1]   No [2]   Can't Say [3]

Do you believe that Orange County Government works efficiently?
    Yes [ ]   No [ ]   Can't Say [ ]

Has Orange County done a good job of balancing growth against environmental concerns?
    Yes [ ]   No [ ]   Can't Say [ ]

Is your household better off financially than one year ago?
    Yes [ ]   No [ ]   Can't Say [ ]

Has Orange County Government done a good job of managing growth?
    Yes [ ]   No [ ]   Can't Say [ ]

Do you watch Orange TV?
    Yes [ ]   No [ ]   Can't Say [ ]

Have you watched Board of County Commission meetings on Orange TV during the last twelve months?
    Yes [ ]   No [ ]   Can't Say [ ]

Have you ever attended a Board of County Commission meeting?
    Yes [ ]   No [ ]   Can't Say [ ]

VI. I will read you some statements. Please tell me whether you Strongly Agree, Agree, Disagree, or Strongly Disagree with the following statements.

	Strongly Agree	Agree	Disagree	Strongly Disagree
I believe that the county government is interested in what I have to say about issues that affect me.	[1]	[2]	[3]	[4]
I know what services the county provides.	[ ]	[ ]	[ ]	[ ]
I rarely contact the county government.	[ ]	[ ]	[ ]	[ ]
The media accurately present county government issues.	[ ]	[ ]	[ ]	[ ]
I have a positive view of Orange County Government.	[ ]	[ ]	[ ]	[ ]
I feel comfortable voicing my opinions to county officials.	[ ]	[ ]	[ ]	[ ]
People in my neighborhood work together to solve their problems.	[ ]	[ ]	[ ]	[ ]
Local schools are doing a good job.	[ ]	[ ]	[ ]	[ ]
Race relations are good in Orange County.	[ ]	[ ]	[ ]	[ ]
I expect economic conditions in Orange County to improve.	[ ]	[ ]	[ ]	[ ]
The economic future looks bright for my household.	[ ]	[ ]	[ ]	[ ]
The quality of life in Orange County is good.	[ ]	[ ]	[ ]	[ ]
I expect the quality of life in Orange County to improve.	[ ]	[ ]	[ ]	[ ]
I expect to be living in Orange County five years from now.	[ ]	[ ]	[ ]	[ ]

VII. Your answers to the following questions will help us better analyze the results of this survey. Let me remind you that you may skip any question you choose not to answer.

What is the zip code of your residence? _____ (number)

Note: The dataset includes the variable "region," which is based on this item.

How long have you lived in Orange County? _____ (number) years

What is your gender?   Male [1]   Female [2]

Do you have children under eighteen years old living at home with you?

Yes [1]   No [2]
If Yes: How many? _____ (number)

Do you rent or own your home?　　　Rent [1]　　Own [2]　　Other [3]

How much formal schooling have you had?

Less than HS	[1]
High School	[2]
Some College	[3]
College Graduate	[4]
Graduate or Professional Degree	[5]

What is your age? ....

18–24	[1]
25–35	[2]
36–45	[3]
46–55	[4]
56–65	[5]
66–75	[6]
76–85	[7]
over 85	[8]

Do you describe yourself as White [1], Black/African-American [2], Hispanic [3], Asian/Pacific Islander [4], Native American [5], or some other ethnic group [6]?

About what is your total annual household income ? _____ dollars
   (Check one.)

$20,000 or less	[1]
$20,001 to $40,000	[2]
$40,001 to $60,000	[3]
$60,001 to $80,000	[4]
above $80,000	[5]

That's all the questions I have. Thank you very much for your help. If you have any questions or comments regarding the survey, you should contact _____ at UCF. Would you like his telephone number again or his email address? By the way, you may get a call from one of my supervisors to check on my performance.

EMPLOYEE ATTITUDES

General Description

The Employee Attitudes dataset includes data from 977 employees of Seminole County Government (Florida). This *general employee survey* can easily be tailored to other research situations. Seminole County is one of five counties in central Florida. One of the smaller counties in terms of area, it includes a mix of very affluent neighborhoods, as well as some rural areas and poor neighborhoods. Human Resources Department staff conducted the survey and visited each county department. Staffs in each department were required to attend a meeting at which the anonymous and voluntary survey was administered; only a few employees chose not to participate in the survey. This is a general employee survey—employees are referred to in this county as "members"—and it includes employee assessments of working conditions, career development, benefits and compensation, supervisory management, customer relations, job skills and training, and satisfaction with Human Resources services. To ensure the anonymity of respondents, surveys were returned in sealed and unmarked envelopes, which were opened by an outside, independent consultant who did the analysis and prepared the final report.

Methods

Considerable care was taken to ensure that the questions were unbiased and consistent with questions typically found in employee surveys. During August 1999, Human Resources Department staff implemented the survey across departments and divisions by assembling all Seminole County Government employees, along with managers, for the purpose of completing the survey. Efforts were made to reach all members, and those unavailable on that day were advised of other opportunities to participate. To ensure the anonymity of members, participants were instructed not to write their name on their survey and to insert the survey into an unmarked white envelope. All envelopes were then delivered to the outside researcher, who opened and analyzed the responses.

A total of 977 surveys were received, or 84.4 percent of the 1,158 total full-time positions with Seminole County. Table W18.1 shows the distribution of these positions by department. A methodological issue is that Seminole County Government chose to state clearly that answering various standard demographic items was "voluntary," which reduced the number of completed responses for these items. The number of completed surveys is shown in Table W18.2. A question arises as to whether the lower response rates for demographic variables may result in any significant *response bias*. To explore this possibility, the aggregate responses of all respondents were compared with the responses of those who answered specific demographic questions. Typically, mean responses should differ by no more than ± 0.03, and no difference should be greater than ± 0.06. To illustrate the analysis, Table W18.3 shows the results of these three questions below, which were selected for their importance or relevance to this concern.

Item 1: "Seminole County is a good place to work for compared to other organizations I know or have worked for."

Item 2: "The quality of service provided to citizens is the same regardless of their race, gender, or background."

Item 3: "My supervisor deals fairly with everyone."

Looking over these data, we can conclude that analyses using the demographic variables are meaningful.

Finally, analysis of the data shows that some departments are quite small and that Seminole County Government has relatively few employees in each of the standard race classifications. For example, only 68 members, or 8.0 percent, of respondents identified themselves as African-American. Likewise, only 37, or 4.4 percent, identified themselves as being of Hispanic origin. The final report does not provide separate reporting for departments with either fewer than 20 respondents or less than a 50 percent response rate. Analyses of department by race contrast Caucasian and non-Caucasian employee perceptions in order to preserve the anonymity of minority respondents in each department.

Table W18.1 ———— Response Rate by Department

DEPARTMENT	Turned in	No. filled full-time positions	Percentage surveyed	Completed responses	Percentage self-identified of full-time positions
Administrative Services	57	57	100	51	89.5
Community Services	27	51	52.9	29	56.8
County Attorney	16	18	88.9	8	44.4
County Manager/BCC Offices	9	10	90	8	80.0
Environmental Services	129	140·	92.1	102	72.8
Fiscal Services	21	21	100	13	61.9
Human Resources	13	13	100	7	53.8
Information Technologies	26	27	96.3	19	70.3
Judicial	18	22	81.8	13	59.1
Library and Leisure Services	132	158	83.5	104	65.8
Planning and Development	108	114	94.7	99	86.8
Public Safety	206	282	73.0	186	65.9
Public Works	212	238	89.1	189	79.4
Tourism	7	7	100	2	28.6
TOTAL	981	1158	85	830	71.7
Unknown				147	
TOTAL				977	

Table W18.2 —⌁⌁— Results from Completed Surveys

Total number of full-time positions:	1,158
Completed responses:	977 (84.4%)
Identification of:	
Gender	865
Race	851
Hispanic origin	832
Pay band	674
Years employed with county	805
Department	830

Table W18.3 —⌁⌁— Mean Answers to Items 1, 2, and 3

		Item 1 (mean)	Item 2 (mean)	Item 3 (mean)
ALL responses		3.64	4.31	3.51
Completed	Gender	3.66	4.33	3.52
	Race	3.64	4.35	3.54
	Hispanic origin	3.65	4.36	3.54
	Pay band	3.67	4.32	3.47
	Years employed	3.66	4.35	3.51
	Department	3.64	4.32	3.52

Detailed Summary

The questions on this survey are consistent with most general employee surveys, which cover many of the same aspects discussed below. The survey instrument has 10 sections designed to assess different aspects of the workplace. The first section measures overall satisfaction with the county as a place to work. The second section assesses a broad range of general working conditions, such as the presence of safety hazards and the manner in which problems are discussed. The third section looks at employee relations with supervisors and management. The fourth section examines how customers are treated. The fifth section focuses on career development. The sixth section assesses cooperation and coordination among departments. The seventh section features questions on the adequacy of job skills and training. The eighth section delves into the quality of Human Resources services and interaction. The ninth section includes two questions about benefits and compensation. The tenth section asks a range of standard demographic questions.

Human Resources Department staff implemented the survey across departments and divisions by assembling all Seminole County Government employees (called "members"), along with managers, during regular work hours for the purpose of completing the survey. An effort was made to reach all members, and those who were unavailable on that day were advised of other opportunities to participate. To ensure the anonymity of members, participants were instructed not to write their name on their survey and to insert the survey into an unmarked white envelope. All envelopes were delivered to the analyst, after which they were opened and analyzed. Out of a total of 1,158 members, 977 returned a usable survey.

Note on Variables

The variables appear in the same order as on the survey instrument. The variable names are limited to eight characters, and the labels are consistent with the survey items. Variable values are indicated on the survey below. Missing values are coded as periods (.) in the dataset. Most items are on a five-point Likert scale.

Students using *SPSS Student Version* software will find additional information relevant to that software on the CD that accompanies this workbook.

Survey Instrument: Seminole County Government Employee Survey

The following questions are designed to assess and improve employee relations. Please evaluate the following statements by checking the appropriate box (mark an "X," please).

SA = Strongly Agree	DK = Don't Know	SD = Strongly Disagree
A = Agree	D = Disagree	

	SA	A	DK	D	SD

1. General Conditions

Overall, I am satisfied with my job at Seminole County......

	5	4	3	2	1

Seminole County is a good place to work compared to other organizations I know about or have worked for .....

Each individual is treated with dignity ....

The morale of Seminole County Government employees is high ....

In general, my department is better to work for than it was two years ago ....

In general, Seminole County Government is a better place to work for than it was two years ago ....

Most days I feel good about coming to work ....

I would proudly recommend Seminole County Government as a good place to work ....

The work that I do is important ....

Our organization welcomes change ....

The County Newsletter is an effective communication tool ...

It is important for the organization to commit to learning about cultural diversity ....

My job is challenging and interesting ....

2. Working Conditions

Problems are discussed openly, candidly, and constructively...

In general, everyone seems to carry his or her fair share of the workload ....

I have a lot of freedom to decide how to do my work ....

	SA	A	DK	D	SD

I seldom feel stressed because of work . . . .

I seldom work late or past my scheduled quitting time . . . . . .

My physical working conditions are reasonable for my
type of work . . . .

The maintenance on the equipment I use is adequate . . . .

Safety hazards in my work area are quickly corrected . . . .

Most of my co-workers are receptive to trying new ways
of conducting business to improve productivity . . . .

My supervisor is skilled and experienced . . . .

3. Supervisory/Management Relations

I feel free to go to a "higher boss" than my immediate
supervisor to discuss any problems that are bothering me . . . .

Senior managers of the organization come through
my work area often . . . .

I have confidence and trust in my supervisor . . . .

My supervisor deals fairly with everyone—does not play
favorites . . . .

My division routinely holds meetings to keep people
informed . . . .

My immediate supervisor helps my work group do its best . . .

Feedback on performance is timely, accurate, and
constructive . . . .

My supervisor and I establish performance goals for the
upcoming year as part of my performance evaluation . . . .

I understand what is expected of me in my job . . . .

SA	A	DK	D	SD

4. Customer Relations

The quality of service provided to citizens is the same regardless of their race, gender, or background . . . .

I feel very confident to make decisions or take action to satisfy our customers. . . . .

The opinions of our customers are important to my work group. . . . .

Most of my co-workers are receptive to trying new ways of conducting business to improve service . . . .

5. Career Management and Rewards

Job opportunities are posted and accessible to me . . . .

When things go well in my job, my contributions are recognized . . . .

The people that get promoted are among the best qualified for the job . . . .

I actively participate and provide input into my performance rating/review . . . .

Our organization has a good performance appraisal system in place . . . .

I am familiar with the Merit Pay Program . . . .

I understand how my performance is evaluated . . . .

I am satisfied with the various member recognition programs . . . .

I understand what I need to do to develop my career with Seminole County Government . . . .

Internal promotions are encouraged here . . . .

6. Cooperation and Coordination

There is cooperation among departments to get the job done . . . .

	SA	A	DK	D	SD

Our organization does a good job of keeping us informed about current developments affecting the organization ......

I understand the organization's vision, mission, goals and values ....

There is a good feeling of teamwork in my work group with people working well together ....

I am aware of my responsibilities and the procedures to follow in resolving a conflict ....

7. Job Skills and Training

Members are given challenging work that provides opportunities to learn new skills ....

Members have the skills to do their work well ....

My performance has improved as a result of attending training programs ....

I receive ongoing training to keep my skills current ....

8. Human Resource Department

The Human Resources staff is accessible and easy to work with..

The Human Resources Department does a good job of representing all employees and acting as a member advocate ....

I am comfortable seeking information and advice from Human Resources ....

I understand how the Employee Assistance Program works and its benefit to me ....

I can use the grievance procedures without fear of retribution

Our Personnel Policies Manual is well-organized and easy to work with..

	SA	A	DK	D	SD

9. Benefits and Compensation

Seminole County's insurance package (health, life, and
optional coverage) meets the needs of employees . . . .

I am paid as well as people in other organizations with similar
jobs . . . .

10. Demographic Questions

Finally, the following questions are asked for the purpose of analysis, only.
Please check the appropriate boxes:

1. What is your gender?

Male	0
Female	1

2. What is your race?

Caucasian	1
African-American	2
Asian or Pacific	3
Native American	4
Other	5

3. Are you of Hispanic origin?

Yes	1
No	2

4. What is your department?

Administrative Services	1
Community Services	2
County Attorney's Office	3
County Manager/BCC	4
Environmental Services	5
Fiscal Services	6
Human Resources	7
Information Technologies	8
Judicial	9
Library & Leisure Services	10
Planning & Development	11
Public Safety	12
Public Works	13
Tourism	14

5. What is your pay band?

Pay Band 1 or 2	1
Pay Band 3 or 4	2
Pay Band 5 or 6	3
Pay Band 7, 8, or 9	4

6. How long have your worked for
   Seminole County Government?

Less than 1 year	1
1+ to 3 years	2
3+ to 5 years	3
5+ to 10 years	4
10+ years	5

COMMUNITY INDICATORS

General Description

The Community Indicators dataset is developed from secondary data sources to provide a profile of cities across the United States. The 98 selected cities include many of the country's largest, as well as those from different states and a few located in rural settings. The data reflect different aspects of interest: demographic, educational, crime, environmental, transportation, sports, economic, and other concerns.

A challenge in gathering this information is that although some data are available at the city level, other data are available only at the county level, and the county boundaries do not always conform to the city boundaries. This is especially the case when data are collected not by the U.S. Census, but by other agencies. When data are collected by the U.S. Census, city estimates are available for demographic, social, educational, and housing data. We identify instances in which data were collected at the county level; many crime and health data are of this nature. In addition, we estimate, based on a visual analysis comparing maps, how well county boundaries match those of the city jurisdictions. In some cases, the fit is quite close, and in other instances it is not.

The main data sources are the U.S. Census, factfinder.census.gov (data from 2004, as available—in a few instances, the census provides only data from the 2000 census). For crime data, see U.S. Department of Justice, Uniform Crime Reporting, www.fbi.gov/ucr/cius_04/offenses_reported/index.html (2004 data). For juvenile crime data, see ojjdp.ncjrs.org/ojstatbb/ezaucr/asp/ucr_display.asp. For health data, see U.S. Department of Health and Human Services, Office on Women's Health, www.healthstatus2010.com/owh/select _variables.aspx (data for men and women are included). Air quality data are from U.S. Environmental Protection Agency, www.epa.gov/air/data/geosel.html. For quality-of-life data, see U.S. Census Bureau, 2002 Economic Census, www.census.gov/econ/census02/guide/02EC_US.HTM.

Definition of Variables

Each variable name appears after its label.

City name—City. This is the city name, as used by the Census.

Caucasian population—Caucasian. The percent of the population that is white.

Number of persons under 18 years—UnderAge18. The number of persons in the city under age 18 years.

Number of persons from 18 through 44—Age18to44. The number of persons in the city with ages 18 through 44 years.

Number of persons from 45 through 64—Age45to64. The number of persons in the city with ages 45 through 64 years.

Number of persons over 65 years—OverAge65. The number of persons in the city over age 65 years.

Total population—Pop. Total population (estimated).

Percent of persons with high school degrees or more—HSGradorHigher. percent of population, over age 25 years, who have a high school degree or higher degrees.

Percent of persons with bachelors degrees or more—BGradorHigher. Percent of population, over 25 years, who have a bachelors degree or higher degrees.

Number of violent crimes—ViolentCrime. The total number of violent crimes. According to Uniform Crime Reporting, violent crimes involve force or threat. There are four types of violent crimes: murder and non-negligent manslaughter, forcible rape, robbery, and aggravated assault. In terms of the rate of offenses for each of the four violent crimes, aggravated assault had the highest rate, estimated at 291.1 offenses per

100,000 inhabitants. There were an estimated 136.7 robberies, 32.2 forcible rapes, and 5.5 murders for each 100,000 resident population in 2004.

Murder and non-negligent manslaughter—Murder. Number of murders and non-negligent manslaughters.

Forcible rape—Rape. Number of forcible rapes.

Burglary—Burglary. Number of burglaries.

Motor vehicle thefts—MotorTheft. Number of motor vehicle thefts.

Full-time law enforcement employees—FTLaw. Number of full-time law enforcement employees.

Performing arts—PerfArts. Number of performing arts companies. Performing arts companies comprise establishments engaged primarily in producing live presentations involving the performances of actors and actresses, singers, dancers, musical groups, and other performing artists.

Museums and historical sites—MusSites. Number of museums or historic sites. Museums are described as establishments engaged primarily in the preservation and exhibition of objects of historical, cultural, and/or educational value. Historical sites are establishments engaged primarily in the preservation and exhibition of sites, buildings, forts, or communities that describe events or persons of particular historical interest.

Spectator sports—Sports. Number of spectator sport teams. Comprises sports teams or clubs participating primarily in live sporting events before a paying audience.

Unemployment rate—Unempl. Unemployment rate (includes some county-level observations).

Household income—Income. Median household income in dollars.

Rentals—Rentals. Number of households that rent.

Management and professional jobs—MgtJobs. Number of jobs in management, professional, and related occupations.

Sales and office jobs—SaleOfficeJobs. Number of jobs in sales and office occupations.

Agriculture and related jobs—AgrJobs. Number of jobs in agriculture, fishing and hunting, and mining.

Construction jobs—ConsJobs. Number of jobs in construction.

Mean travel time to work—TravelTime. Mean travel time to work (in minutes) for workers ages 16 years and older.

Use of public transportation—PublicTrans. People using public transportation for going to work, excluding taxicabs. Workers ages 16 years and older.

County-based measures:

Juvenile crime—CountyJuvCrime. Total number of juvenile crimes committed in the county. Includes violent crimes, property crimes, and nonindex crimes such as alcohol violations, forgery, fraud, and various other crimes.

Death rate—CountyDeath. Death rate in the county (2002 data).

Infant mortality rate—CountyInfant. Infant mortality rate per 100,000 population, 1996–2000.

AIDS cases—CountyAIDS. Number of AIDS cases in the county (2002 data).

Cancer cases—CountyCancer. Number of cancer cases in the county (2002 data).

Match between city and county—CityCountyMatch. Our assessment of how well the county boundaries match city boundaries. 1 = close, 2 = fair, 3 = dissimilar.

Air quality index—Air. The Air Quality Index (AQI) is an index for reporting daily air quality. The Environmental Protection Agency calculates the AQI for five major air pollutants regulated by the Clean Air Act: ground-level ozone, particle pollution (also known as particulate matter), carbon monoxide, sulfur dioxide, and nitrogen dioxide. The AQI runs from 0 to 500. The higher the AQI value, the greater the level of air pollution and the greater the health concern.

Air quality data source—AirSource. Some data are from cities; others are from counties. This variable shows the source of the AQI data only. 1 = MSA (metropolitan statistical area), 2 = county.

Counties—Counties. Counties included in the county-based measures.

WATERSHED

General Description
The Watershed dataset was developed from rating variables, explanations, descriptions, and specific data incorporated within the Environmental Protection Agency's (EPA's) Index of Watershed Indicators (IWI) Web site (www.epa.gov/iwi). The IWI is a compilation score determined by combining the impact of 16 measured variables used as indicators of general watershed conditions for more than 2,262 watersheds within the United States and Puerto Rico. These indicators measure the general condition of the nation's rivers, streams, wetlands, and estuaries.

Background
The 16 variables contained within the IWI are divided into two groups. The first seven variables collectively are termed *condition indicators,* and taken together they represent existing conditions of the specific watershed. (Below are the variable labels. The actual variable names appear later.) These seven condition indicators consist of "designated use attainment," "fish and wildlife consumption advisories," "drinking water impairment," "sediment contamination," "ambient water quality for four toxic pollutants," "ambient water quality for four conventional pollutants," and a "wetlands loss index" developed from two separate wetlands loss inventories. The remaining nine variables comprise the *vulnerability indicators,* which evaluate the potential for future degradation of a particular watershed. These vulnerability indicators are "aquatic/wetlands species at risk," "toxic pollutant loads discharged exceeding aggregate state permit allowance," "conventional pollutant loads discharged exceeding aggregate state permit allowance," "urban runoff potential," "index of agricultural runoff potential," "population change within the watershed," "hydrologic modifications to the watershed," "estuarine pollution susceptibility index," and an "atmospheric deposition factor." Condition indicators and vulnerability indicators are combined, yielding an IWI rating for the specific watershed.

This dataset contains four additional variables. They are the "overall watershed characteristic score," "geographical region," "population of the watershed as of the 1990 national census," and a variable describing the "wetlands loss index."

The 122 watershed observations comprising this dataset consist of two select groups of observations. First, 96 watersheds throughout the United States were specifically identified by the National Sediment Inventory as containing "Areas of Probable Concern" (www.epa.gov/OST/Events/sedlist.html). Second, an additional 26 watershed observations—chosen from sparsely populated, remote areas throughout the United States—were selected to provide comparison data for the 96 observations noted as Areas of Probable Concern. They were verified to be nonduplicative, meaning that no watershed is listed twice within the dataset. It bears comment that finding watersheds in the continental United States without some indicated degree of impairment, or expressed concern relating to their overall rating, is a difficult task.

According to the EPA, the IWI shows that 15 percent of our watersheds nationally have relatively good water quality, 36 percent have moderate problems, 22 percent have more serious water quality problems, and 27 percent cannot be characterized because of lack of information. Nationally, 1 in 15 is also highly vulnerable to further degradation.

Variable summaries provided below are intended to convey a practical understanding of the nature of each variable and why it constitutes a parameter of concern with regard to overall watershed conditions. The data collection processes inherent in the development of the IWI database involved coordination and cooperation between federal, state, tribal, and private organizations. The indicators are based on existing, published data sources collected as part of monitoring state water resources. EPA compiles existing information on the quantity, chemical and physical composition, and geographic location of indicators shown below. Complete information addressing the collection of raw data, selection and development of variables, access to the data collection procedures and sources, and an evaluation of threshold criteria is available through the EPA IWI Web site.

Summary of Individual Variables: Condition Indicators
Each variable name appears after its label.

Watershed characteristic—Wshedch. This overall evaluation describes the condition of aquatic resources for a specific watershed.

Designated use attainment—Useatnmn. This variable is the percentage of water sources within a specific watershed evaluated as meeting the requirements and conditions to fully support the water source's designated uses.

Fish and wildlife consumption advisories—Advisory. When excessive levels of toxic substances are identified within watershed species, states may issue advisories warning against using specific species as a food source. These advisories may be targeted at specific population groups such as the elderly, small children, or pregnant women. This variable is the number of advisories issued within the watershed advising against the consumption of fish or aquatic wildlife. This variable is considered to be a good indicator of the general condition of a watershed and of the extent of toxic substance buildup within a watershed food chain.

Drinking water impairment—Wtrimprd. This variable provides a partial indicator of the condition of water sources within the watershed that could potentially constitute a source of drinking water. These potential sources include both ground and surface water sources sampled prior to treatment or purification for use as drinking water.

Contaminated sediments—Sedicont. This variable is a measure of the potential risks to human health and the environment determined through chemical analysis of bottom sediments, sediment toxicity data, and fish tissue residue data.

Ambient water quality (toxic pollutants)—Toxicon. This variable measures the presence and amount of copper, chromium (hexavalent), nickel, and zinc within watershed water sources. This database continues to the next data layer that provides an actual percentage of samples taken exceeding allowed levels.

Ambient water quality (conventional pollutants)—Conpolut. This variable measures the presence and amount of ammonia, dissolved oxygen, phosphorus, and pH within watershed water sources. This database continues to the next data layer providing an actual percentage of samples taken exceeding allowed levels.

Wetland loss index—Wtlds92 and Wtlnlos2. By combining two indicators, this variable measures the amount of cumulative and continuing wetlands lost. The National Resources Inventory indicates the percentage of watershed wetlands lost during the period of 1982 to 1992, while the National Wetlands

Inventory estimates the percentage of watershed wetlands lost from the 1780s to the 1980s. While these two measures are combined to a single index for use within the IWI, this database continues to the next data layer and splits them back out to individual measures, Wtlds92, and Wtlnlos2, respectively. The two individual measures provide a better indication of the extent of historical wetlands loss.

Summary of Individual Variables: Vulnerability Indicators

Aquatic/wetlands species at risk—Speatrsk. This indicator represents the number of species documented in a watershed that are classified by the Heritage Network as being critically imperiled and assesses the conservation of plant and animal species at the greatest risk of extinction within the watershed.

Pollution loads discharged beyond permit limits (toxic)—Toxdisc. Within the IWI database, this variable is listed as an aggregate index by individual state. If the total toxic pollutant discharges within the state did not exceed the total amount allowed by all permits cumulatively, then the watershed was not considered at risk. This database continues to the next data layer and documents the actual number of incidents in which individual permit discharge limits have been exceeded.

Pollution loads discharged beyond permit levels (conventional)—Convdisc. Within the IWI database, this variable is listed as an aggregate index by individual state. If the total conventional pollutant discharges within the state did not exceed the total amount allowed by all permits cumulatively, then the watershed was not considered at risk. This database continues to the next data layer and documents the actual number of incidents in which individual permit discharge limits have been exceeded.

Urban runoff potential—Urbnrnof. This variable is an indicator of the percentage of a watershed consisting of impervious surfaces (roads, paved parking lots, roofs, and so on). As the amount of impervious surfaces within a watershed increases as a result of development, natural flow patterns and volumes within streams and rivers can be altered significantly, leading to an increased potential for flooding and an increased potential for runoff of pollutants such as fertilizers and insecticides, in turn leading to further degradation of water sources within the watershed.

Agricultural runoff potential—Agrirnof. Nitrogen runoff potential from fertilizers, pesticide runoff, and sediment delivery to streams and rivers are combined in this index variable. The value for a particular watershed is ranked among 2,110 watersheds evaluated for this variable.

Population change—Popuincr. Comparison of national census data from 1980 and 1990 determined the percentage of population increase within a watershed. Increasing populations place additional burdens on watershed environments through the impact of continued development, increased exploitation of available water sources, further loss of wetlands, increased sewage flow, and additional impervious surfaces.

Hydrological modifications—Hydromod. This index is a measure of the relative amount of reservoir impoundment volume within a watershed. Dams alter natural river and stream flow rates and, when built, can lead to the loss of wetlands. Also, as water accumulates behind the dam, the resulting lake or impoundment can serve as a repository for runoff pollutant introduction, concentration, and subsequent sediment contaminant buildup.

Estuarine pollution susceptibility—Polusucp. Measuring an estuary's susceptibility to contaminant introduction and pollution buildup, this indicator is defined as an estuary's relative vulnerability to concentrations of dissolved and particulate substances. Coastal lands continue to be developed as population densities continue to shift to these regions. It should be noted that a value of "4" for this variable indicates no estuary present within the watershed for evaluation.

Atmospheric deposition—Atmosdep. Nitrogen is a primary nutrient that can cause algae blooms and other problems within watershed water sources. Atmospheric deposition primarily through precipitation is a significant source of nitrogen to these water sources. The units are kilograms per hectare per year. (One kilogram equals approximately 2.2 pounds; one hectare is 100 by 100 meters square, and approximately equal to 2.47 acres.)

Watershed population—Wtrshpop. These are the population figures as of the 1990 census.

Geographical region—Region. This is the location of the watershed within the continental United States:

> *Northeast:* Maine, Massachusetts, New Jersey, New York, Rhode Island
>
> *Southeast:* Alabama, Florida, Georgia, Kentucky, Louisiana, Mississippi, North Carolina, South Carolina, Tennessee
>
> *Midwest:* Illinois, Indiana, Kansas, Michigan, Minnesota, Missouri, Ohio, Wisconsin
>
> *Northwest:* Idaho, Montana, North Dakota, Oregon, South Dakota, Utah, Washington
>
> *Southwest:* California, Texas
>
> ***Methodological Note:*** Classified as "Northeast" are one watershed at the joint boundaries of Pennsylvania, Maryland, and West Virginia; one watershed at the joint boundaries of New York, Ohio, and Pennsylvania; and one watershed at the joint boundaries of Ohio, Pennsylvania, and West Virginia. Classified as "Southeast" is one watershed at the joint boundaries of Arkansas, Kentucky, Mississippi, Missouri, and Tennessee.

PRODUCTIVITY

General Description

This dataset contains hypothetical data about a government organization. It was created to illustrate interrelationships between employee perceptions of their work; organizational environment; and work-center, departmental, and overall organization productivity. Such data are usually obtained through employee surveys and internal administrative reports of departmental productivity.

Background

Biltrite Shipbuilding and Marine Repair is a small government shipbuilding and marine vessel repair facility located in Charleston, South Carolina. The organizational workforce is comprised primarily of federal General Schedule (GS) and Wage Grade (WG) employees. During the 1980s, Biltrite specialized in the manufacture of small coastal patrol and riverine vessels for the United States Army and the United States Coast Guard. During the 1990s the organization was involved primarily with repair of existing craft, with virtually no new construction contracts.

While Biltrite was able to remain economically viable during this period, the organization was subjected to a series of Reduction in Force (RIF) personnel actions. These RIFs resulted in a 31 percent personnel cutback over seven years. Biltrite accomplished the required cutbacks through normal employee attrition, normal retirement, and early retirement incentives. After an extended period of government defense-spending cutbacks and facilities closures, Biltrite Shipbuilding and Marine Repair now anticipates a resurgence of government military building contracts. To ensure that Biltrite is positioned as competitively as possible, the company reviewed its past productivity evaluations and compared them with those of its competition. While Biltrite's productivity does not lag behind industry averages, Biltrite does not stand out as an industry leader.

Biltrite is now evaluating alternative productivity improvement strategies, which will enhance its opportunities of being awarded future government contracts. As part of this effort, Biltrite contracted with Deeterman & Associates, a recognized leader in productivity studies within the industry. Deeterman evaluated all 10 Biltrite work centers with its four departments (see Figure W18.1).

Deeterman personnel performed the overall organizational study over a period of two months. Individual employee interviews were performed during a two-week period. All 321 Biltrite employees below the senior management level were interviewed. The survey instrument utilized was designed to assess multiple contributing aspects of three index variables and three single concept variables. Additionally, data were collected on length of employment with Biltrite and number of workdays missed because of illness over the past 12 months.

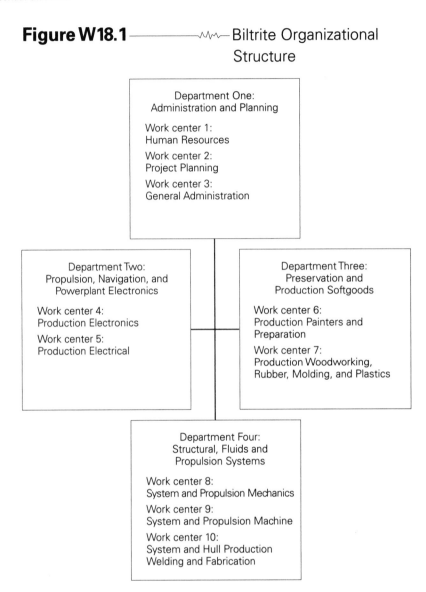

Figure W18.1————–⌁⌁⌁—Biltrite Organizational Structure

Summary of Variables

To measure the different aspects of employee satisfaction, Deeterman personnel used a seven-point Likert scale, ranging from "Strongly Disagree" to "Strongly Agree." Index variables were formed by averaging the responses to items with strong item-to-total and inter-item correlations. All variables were rescaled on a 10-point scale in which 1 = low and 10 = high.

The 12 variables studied here are listed by variable name and include the variable type and the corresponding statements from the survey.

Jobknowl. Single variable. Type: continuous. The statement evaluated by the respondent: "I have adequate skills and knowledge to perform my job."

Wkrtrtmt. Single variable. Type: continuous. The statement evaluated by the respondent: "At Biltrite, I am treated fairly and with respect."

Teamwork. An index variable (Cronbach alpha = 0.81). Type: continuous. The statements evaluated by the respondents were:

"In my work center, teams are used effectively to accomplish job assignments."

"I am satisfied with the functioning of my work team."

"People from different work centers work well together to accomplish job assignments."

"People from different departments work well together to accomplish job assignments."

Jobauthr. Single variable. Type: continuous. The statement evaluated by the respondent: "I have adequate decision-making authority to do my job well."

Recogawd. An index variable (Cronbach alpha = 0.74). Type: continuous. The statements evaluated by the respondents were:

"On a day-to-day basis I understand what is expected of me by my supervisors."

"In my work center, supervisors' expectations of worker performance are fair."

"In my department, employee recognition and performance cash incentives are awarded fairly."

"People in other departments don't have to work as hard as I do to receive the same recognition or performance cash awards."

"Work done excellently is recognized at Biltrite."

Wrkdyssk. Number of workdays missed because of illness during the last twelve months. Type: continuous.

Inthempl. Length of time as Biltrite employee. Type: continuous.

Workcntr. Employee's work center. Type: categorical.

Productivity. An index variable (Cronbach alpha = 0.78). Type: continuous. The statements evaluated by the respondents were:

"In my work center, employees are motivated to work."

"The productivity of my work center is high."

"Work activities are well planned."

"My supervisor is always available to help keep projects on track."

"We are always customer oriented."

Wkctrpro. Work-center productivity determined by Deeterman & Associates by examining past work-center performance data, including production planning, material procurement, availability of needed material, materials expended, man-hours scheduled and expended per production task, total and job-specific overtime man-hours expended, and percentage of production tasks requiring rework. These values were then weighted and compared with industry standards. Type: continuous.

Dprtment. The department employee's work center is located within. Type: categorical.

Deptprod. Department productivity determined by Deeterman & Associates. Type: continuous.

CRIME

General Description

This time series dataset includes data from a fictional upper midwestern U.S. metropolitan area, with a population of approximately 1 million residents. It was created to approximate the juvenile crime rate and trends in that rate, as documented by the Office of Juvenile Justice and Delinquency Prevention (OJJDP) from 1990 to 1998 (*OJJDP Statistical Briefing Book,* which can be found online at ojjdp.ncjrs.org/ojstatbb/qa260.html).

The metropolitan area known as Normalton is representative of national population demographic averages. The juvenile population is estimated by applying age distributions obtained from the *Statistical Abstract of the United States, 1998,* 118th edition. Juvenile arrest data contained within this dataset represent the average number of juvenile criminal arrests per 100,000 juveniles. Juveniles are defined as being male or female, 10 to 17 years of age.

Arrests for juvenile curfew violations are not contained within the juvenile criminal arrest variables. Rather, they are represented within the specific curfew violation arrest variable Curfviol.

Unemployment figures averaged over the year represent national rates obtained from the Bureau of Labor Statistics. A variation was inserted to represent the hiring practices associated with areas that evidence a seasonal tourist economic component.

Background

In June 1993 the city council of Normalton and the newly elected mayor, the Honorable I. M. Worthyman, received from the chief of police the annual report on Normalton crime. The report indicated that, as in the rest of the nation, juvenile crime in Normalton had continued to rise. This report lent further support to an identified upward trend in juvenile crime that began in 1989.

In July 1993 an Australian family was violently attacked and robbed outside their Normalton hotel by a gang of youths. Their daughter was paralyzed as a result of the injuries received during the attack. This family represented only 5 of the typical 1.2 million tourists drawn to Normalton each spring, summer, and fall by its widely heralded natural beauty, ecological diversity, and three world-class roller coaster theme parks. The case drew national attention.

Feeling that the city must take action to halt what was perceived as an upwardly spiraling juvenile crime rate, the mayor and city council proposed a strict juvenile curfew. Following a survey of city residents, which indicated broad support for the initiative, the city council drafted and unanimously passed a juvenile curfew to take effect on January 1, 1994. The curfew affected all juveniles between the ages of 10 and 17, requiring them to be off the streets between the hours of 8 PM and 1 AM, unless they were in transit to or from an official recreational event or a church function, or were accompanied by an adult. All juveniles were required to be at home after 1 AM.

The city council also passed a parental responsibility law, whereby parents found negligent in exercising proper control and supervision of their children could be held legally responsible for their children's legal transgressions, including curfew violations. This law took effect on March 1, 1994.

By 1999 there were questions about the effectiveness of the curfew, as the mayor was preparing to run for another term.

Explanation of Variables

The listing below shows the variable names, a brief definition of each of the variables, and the variable type. The dataset also includes the first-order differences of these variables, shown as Crimar_1, Juvars_1, Curfi_1, Parenr_1, Curfew_1, Juvnco_1, and Unempl_1.

Crimarst. Number of total juvenile criminal arrests by month from January 1, 1990, through December 31, 1998. Type: continuous.

Juvarsts. Number of monthly juvenile criminal arrests between 8 PM and 1 AM, January 1, 1990, through December 31, 1998. Type: continuous.

Curfviol. Total juvenile arrests for curfew violations, by month. Type: continuous.

Policcur. Number of police per shift dedicated to juvenile code enforcement. Type: continuous.

Month. Month of year. Type: categorical.

Month. A dummy variable of each month. For example, Month1 denotes January, Month2 denotes February, and so forth. Type: categorical.

Befraftr. Number of daily juvenile criminal arrests between 8 PM and 1 AM 54 days before and 54 days after implementing juvenile curfew restrictions. Type: continuous.

Parenrsp. Number of parents held legally responsible for their children's violations. Type: continuous.

Unemploy. Percentage of Normalton labor force unemployed. Type: continuous.

Juvncort. Juvenile criminal cases adjudicated in juvenile court. Type: continuous.

TIME

General Description

All of the variables in the Time dataset are hypothetical. The dataset was developed to illustrate problems relating to simple and multiple regression, as discussed in Chapters 13 and 15 of the textbook. The Time dataset is used for exercises in Chapters 13 and 15 of this workbook. Specifically, these exercises deal with the following problems:

1. Identifying and removing outliers
2. Performing regression with dummy variables
3. Nonlinear relations among variables
4. Autocorrelation

Each problem is associated with a different exercise, and the variables associated with each exercise are defined in the next section.

Summary of Variables

The dataset contains four different sets of variables:

1. Two variables, Fishcon and Contam1, represent measurements taken from different parts of a large lake in order to test the hypothesis that alleged water pollution is affecting the stock of certain fish.
   Fishcon = The concentration of fish.
   Contam1 = The concentration of a water pollutant.

2. The Time dataset also contains observations from 35 hypothetical cities regarding the use of citizen focus groups in various departments (Focus). The data are based on a survey. Most variables are index variables taken from different survey questions. The variables are defined as follows:
   Focus = A composite measure of the breadth and depth of the use of citizen focus groups in a city. Varies from 0 (low) to 20 (high).
   Mgrint = A measure of the city manager's interest in obtaining citizen-based feedback. Varies from 1 (low) to 4 (high).
   Pubcompl = A measure of public complaints about the quality and effectiveness of a wide range of municipal services. Varies from 1 (low) to 8 (high).
   Budget = Indicates whether municipal budgets have increased in the past two years. Values: −1 = decrease in budget; 0 = no change in budget; 1 = increase in budget.
   Size = City size. Varies from 1 = small to 7 = large.
   Region = An indicator variable of the region in which the city is located. Values: 1 = Northeast; 2 = South; 3 = Midwest; 4 = West.

3. It is commonly hypothesized that crimes are more frequent in large cities. The dataset contains the following variables:
   Nvcrime = Index of nonviolent crimes in a given year.
   Citysize = City size.

4. Time series data are common in program evaluation and public policy. These variables examine the impact of a law, which, among other things, increases jail time for driving under the influence (DUI). The dataset contains the following variables:
   Fatal = Traffic fatalities per 100,000 miles driven.
   Year = Year of traffic fatalities measured.
   Short = A dummy variable identifying when the policy intervention occurred, namely, in 1980 when a law was passed that requires mandatory jail time for DUI. Values: 0 = pre-law adoption (pre-1980), and 1 = post-law adoption (post-1980).
   Long = A dummy variable identifying the number of years of post-policy adoption. Values: 0 = for pre-law adoption, 1 = for 1980, 2 = for 1981, 3 = for 1982, and so forth. This variable gives weight to long-term effects of policy.
   Jailtime = Days of jail time served by offenders because of the law.